STEADFAST
CHRISTIAN

STEADFAST CHRISTIAN

A HIGHER CALL TO FAITH, FAMILY, AND HOPE

PATRICK DILLON

Steadfast Christian,
LLC, Durango,
Colorado

The opinions expressed in this book are strictly the thoughts of the principle author, Patrick Dillon, and in no way are these thoughts officially endorsed by any person(s), entity, company, or organization used as a reference (source) in this publication. Following any advice, opinions, or suggestions by the author, Patrick Dillon, will be completely at your own discretion.

Warning – Some internet sites may contain viruses or other harmful content that may cause harm to your computer or other electronic devices. Therefore, opening any suggested internet sites recommended or listed as a source in this book will be completely at your own risk. The author, Patrick Dillon, or any other party participating or referred to in this book, including the owner(s) of the internet site(s) from where the potential harm may come from, will not be liable for any damages that may result.

Psalm 51:10

*Create in me a pure heart, O God, and
renew a steadfast spirit within me.*

Dedications

This book is dedicated to my dad and grandpa whom I love dearly and miss every day. I look forward to our reunion in Heaven.

Dad

Grandpa

Contents

Acknowledgements

This would not have been possible without the support and patience of my beloved wife and best friend. "What do you think about this or what do you think about that?" over and over again. It has been enough to drive her crazy. Without her editing skills, this book would have never made it through the publishing process. I can't thank her enough and will always be grateful for her help and I love her more than words can describe.

And to my son whom I admire more than anyone else, for his wisdom and steadfast conviction in staying out of trouble, even during his high school years. He has been a wonderful role model for our entire family and to his peers. His photo editing skills enabled him to successfully restore several damaged family pictures with one dating back over 100 years ago. Future generations will thank him for his hard work to help preserve our family heritage. He has taught me invaluable lessons on a number of occasions and I love him dearly.

I thank my Mom and Grandma for praying so hard for me throughout the years. I know this is the main reason why I'm a Christian today.

To my brother and sister for their encouraging words and support in a challenging world. To my uncles who are/were there for me during the tough periods in my life. They always seem to have the right words I need to hear. To the rest of my family for their continued support and generosity. I thank God for the wonderful blessing of family and may Christ richly bless them all.

My most sincere thanks to God for saving me time and time again. He picks me up whenever I fall and comforts me in my time of need. He is my strength, my confidante, my entire life. I love Him with all my heart. Thanks to: Biblica US, Inc. for giving me permission to use the *New International Version* (NIV®) for all the bible verses used in this book.

Leo Severino and all at Metanoia Films, LLC for permission to use their website link and for mentioning the producer in one of my stories. I admire their steadfast dedication to helping save the unborn and their positive influence on society with the production of uplifting films.

Merriam-Webster Online Dictionary, Reasons to Believe, Saturday Evening Post magazine, LifeGaurd, United Americans for Life Action (AUL Action), Thesaurus.com, authors of *The Privileged Planet*, and to all the other sources that I have cited in this book.

Isaiah for a picture taken only a few miles above Grandpa's goldmine where he was caught in a rainstorm and had to find his way back to camp in complete darkness.

Marc Adamus for the use of his front cover photograph, "Beautiful Day," taken early in the morning capturing a breathtaking scene of the magnificent Rocky Mountains.

Introduction

God is Real!

The phrase, "It takes one to know one," is the foundation upon which I have written this book. I'm the last person who should be talking about righteous living. While attending high school, it literally took a brief apparition from Heaven while in deep prayer to snap me out of my downward spiral. The vision only lasted a few seconds with nothing said, but it was powerful enough to change my life forever. The change didn't happen overnight and it is still continuing on a daily basis. Without God's intervention and prayer from family members, my life would have been a complete disaster. Only God is perfect and only by following His Word can I say anything that is good. No matter who we are, whether we're rich, middle class, homeless, or somewhere in between, we need to follow the teachings of Christ to avoid going through unnecessary hardship as individuals and as a nation.

I've often felt convicted, hypocritical, and at times, self righteous while writing this book because I know that I am a sinner and have committed almost every type of sin discussed here. But while in prayer, God reminded me that I couldn't wait until I was good enough because that day on Earth would never come. I will always have to completely rely on Jesus for everything – I'm not good enough, but Christ's grace and strength within me is.

Praise God for loving all of us so personally and for caring for our every need. Jesus has empowered us with His love and has commissioned each one of us to proclaim His Holy Word. Even with this in mind, I often feel helpless as the world continues its slide towards immorality and the sad thing is – I am contributing to this decline. After finally realizing that my complaining wasn't helping anyone, I decided to do something about it and felt compelled to write this book.

I believe we have come to a point in history where the existence of true Christianity is literally at stake. We have watered down our faith to become more acceptable to society. While the secular world is working overtime to destroy Christian values, some of us are blindly stumbling along, falling deeper into the abyss of secularism and avarice. Our slide has not gone unnoticed and the alarm has already been sounded by many Christians – but are we listening?

I'm not saying that everything in our world is evil; rather, there is still a lot of good. Healthcare workers are saving lives, people are helping others in their time of need, businesses are providing us with essential goods and services, schools are preparing our young and adults for new careers, government is trying to make sure that law and order is maintained and that our country is protected from our enemies that want to harm us, and last but not least, religious organizations are providing us with a common place to worship our Lord together. However, evil is present and we can get ourselves into a lot of trouble if we're not careful. As Christians, the only way we can steer clear and keep from becoming part of the problem is to constantly rely on our Lord's strength to help us become steadfast followers of Christ.

Update – April 20, 2009

When I first started writing this book in 2006, it seemed a little strange to be writing about troubled times when the economy appeared to have rebounded nicely from the 9/11 terrorist attacks. Prosperity was in the headlines, at least for Wall Street and the corporate world. However, I was not focusing on material wealth back then just as I am not in the first months of 2009. Instead, I continue to focus on the spiritual health of our nation. But wow, what a difference a few years can make! Today, our economy is in shambles and fear and uncertainty have gripped our nation and the world. I wasn't surprised when it became apparent that greed and immorality were the main ingredients in this self-inflicted recession.

Special Note – The chapters in this book had mostly been written before this financial crisis took place. Therefore, I have recently added chapter 9 to further elaborate on what is now commonly referred to as "the great recession" of 2008/2009. I have also added updates (Update – . . .) throughout the rest of the chapters in this book to include more recent events that occurred after I had already written the chapters.

The recent events have put a new sense of urgency to my work. The moral and economic collapse of our world has happened a lot faster than I had imagined. It appears that we are literally witnessing the systematic breakdown of society, a society that has chosen to turn a blind eye to God. If the world doesn't change from its ways by coming back to our Lord, our downward spiral will only continue to accelerate. However, as Christians, we cannot let this destroy our hope and joy because we have an all powerful and loving Creator who will look after us in every situation no matter how bad or good things become.

In other words, we have to focus on God's power, not on the world's problems. In fact, if we look at our present times and throughout history, most every culture that suffered moral breakdown ended in failure. To me this is just further proof that God is real. When we follow His ways, the world becomes a better place, but when we turn away from Him, the world falls apart. Therefore, it is crucial that we humble ourselves and ask our Almighty God for help.

While writing this book, my wife has frequently reminded me that I have been guilty of a lot of things written here. I reminded her that no one needs this more than I do. I don't think she fully understands what is driving me and I really don't have all the answers either. I do know that something deep within has snapped me out of my complacency, resulting in an urgent need to get my thoughts down on paper. Maybe it's because I personally struggle so much in keeping God's Word that I think everyone else has the same problem. Whatever the reason, I have often felt guilty when not spending enough time on this book and I have been plagued with distractions making it difficult to progress. It has been like being on a boat that is taking on water where I'm bailing frantically with one hand and writing this with the other. Because of the recent change of events with the world's economy collapsing, I am now convinced that God has put this in my heart because He already knew beforehand what was coming and knows that our only hope is to follow Him. I've seen this same message coming from many Christians because the Holy Spirit is revealing this to all who will listen. **(End of update)**

† † †

After publishing this book I will probably receive ridicule from others, especially those who know me best because they have personally witnessed me committing some of the things that I have discouraged others from doing. Regardless, this is not about me; rather, the focus should be on how each of our own lives are measuring up to God's Word. Therefore, I won't have any hard feelings if this occurs. The recovered alcoholic or drug addict is usually more effective in helping those afflicted because they have a much better understanding of what the person is going through. With experience comes wisdom. I have never taken any drugs but the use of alcohol is a different story.

I learned the hard way that choosing the wrong path will only harm your life and those around you. You don't have to go through hell to find God and it is my deepest hope and prayer that anyone who reads this book, especially youth, will learn not to repeat some of my own and my family's personal experiences that separated us from God. I also hope others will follow the good examples that are portrayed here in the form of family stories (a memoir, past and present).

The main message in this book is hope – the kind of hope that can only come from God. Sin in our world has left many of us, including Christians, confused and without direction making us more vulnerable to the secular pressures of society. The answer to this moral crisis is clear – prayer, fasting, and reconciliation in our own hearts and with our brothers and sisters in Christ. In order for this to be accomplished, we need a steadfast, conscious belief in God. Contrary to worldly belief, there is nothing in the universe that can bring us true happiness except through Him. As Christians, we need to love, support, convict, and encourage one another instead of tearing each other down through slanderous gossip and religious bickering (we're right and you're wrong). (Ephesians 4:32)

> Be kind and compassionate to one another, forgiving
> each other, just as in Christ God forgave you.

We cannot stand divided; instead, we have to find common ground through the holy teachings of our Lord. When we open our eyes, we can see the negative results caused in part by our lukewarm behavior. Sin is prevalent in every corridor of society – in the media, our homes, our schools, at work, in sports, and even in our churches. Some of our ministers and priests are falling into moral disparity and marriages are failing at an all time high which have contributed to the spiritual and moral demise of our families. How far must we fall before we take this crisis serious enough to get on our knees and repent? Scripture tells us that we are all one body; therefore, we are all affected by sin and share in the responsibility of its consequences. This doesn't mean we should live in fear because the world is not in control – our loving Father is. The Apostle Paul confirms this in 2 Timothy 1:7.

> *For God did not give us a spirit of timidity, but a spirit of power, of love and of self-discipline.*

If we take this scripture to heart, we have the power through Christ Jesus to change our lives for the better, but if we continue to ignore our present dilemma, we only have ourselves to blame. Choosing God does not mean our lives will not be without trials; rather, our Lord will give us the necessary strength to endure them. This is a comforting thought in a troubled world.

Although I used stories from my family's lives to express certain points, I did not reveal personal details such as the names, locations, and religious backgrounds of the people discussed here. It is my hope to elevate this discussion above the walls of religious denominations allowing Christians to come together from all walks of life. The primary purpose for writing this book was/is to fulfill a heavy burden in my heart. It is my hope and prayer that God might be glorified through this amateur attempt to express His divine Word.

My inspiration came from my deceased dad and grandpa to whom I have dedicated this book.

Chapter 1

Obstacles That Separate Us From God

Why Do We Believe?

The word "Christian" is defined in the Online Merriam-Webster Dictionary as, "One who professes belief in the teachings of Jesus Christ."[1] Is it easier for us to profess our belief in words or through action? Is one more important than the other or are they both equally important to truly express our faith? If we say we believe, the next question would be to what degree? Are we **steadfast** in our belief?

Below is a partial list of words used as synonyms for steadfast found at Thesaurus.com:

> abiding, allegiant, changeless, constant, firm, fixed, loyal, never-failing, persevering, reliable, resolute, stable, steady, stubborn, sure, true,

---

1 "Christian." Merriam-Webster Online Dictionary. 2009. Merriam-Webster Online. 21 September 2007.
<http://www.merriam-webster.com/dictionary/christian>.
By permission. From the Merriam-Webster Online Dictionary © 2009 by Merriam- Webster, Incorporated. <www.merriam-web.com>.

unbending, unfaltering, unflinching, unmovable, unquestioning, unwavering, wholehearted[2]

It would be nice if Christians could live up to all the above words on a daily basis but unfortunately, we fall short. It doesn't mean we should stop trying because it is not by our strength that we do this; rather, it is Christ Jesus whom we rely on for everything in our lives. Living a steadfast Christian life may sound boring to some but this is quite to the contrary. In reality, we cannot have lasting joy unless we are steadfast in our belief in Christ. God created us with a desire in our hearts that only He can fulfill and until we realize this, our lives will not be complete.

As Christians, why do we believe in something we cannot see, touch, hear, or for that matter even fully understand? It is difficult to believe in something that seems too good to be true, but to our eternal benefit, God really does exist and He loves us more than we could ever imagine. Most of us come to the knowledge there is a God from our parents and later through the church, friends, and others. As children, belief in something we couldn't see came easily as did our belief in the Tooth Fairy, Santa Claus, and the Easter Bunny. I know when I was a child, I wanted to do more than just believe in God – I wanted to feel Him. On numerous occasions after church, I would go outside and clap my hands together rapidly without actually touching them, and after a moment, it gave the effect that something was between them. In front of everyone I yelled out, "I've got Jesus in my hands!"

On another occasion after listening to a sermon on faith, I remembered the words, "With faith in God, anything is possible." I took this very seriously, and immediately after church, I ran outside and started flapping my arms up and down as hard as I could, begging Jesus to allow me to fly. This had always been my childhood dream and I thought for sure it was finally coming true.

---

2 "Steadfast." Roget's 21st Century Thesaurus, Third Edition. Philip Lief Group 2009. 21 August 2007. Thesaurus.com
<http://thesaurus.reference.com/browse/steadfast>.

After awhile I began to tire and realized it wasn't going to happen. Making a fool out of myself didn't bother me, but not being able to fly did. I remember feeling a little angry with God because of it.

At a certain age, we have to make a distinction between what is real and what is fantasy. If we are fortunate enough to come from a Christian home, this distinction can be more easily derived, but not without its difficulties. Prior to attending school, we tended to believe everything our parents told us. As we enter school, however, we start to learn things that may be contrary to what we have come to believe. This is especially true in today's society. In the classroom, God cannot be mentioned in a religious connotation with the exception of the Pledge of Allegiance, and recently, even our sacred pledge has come under attack. Rather than learning biblical teachings of creation, most children are taught at an early age that they are a byproduct of evolution. It is unfortunate that Evolution has become the world's official scientific solution for all the unknown mysteries that mankind has yet to comprehend.

The following items addressed in this chapter may seem like ordinary common sense, but it is the ordinary things we do in life that have the most impact on our faith. Unfortunately, we are turning a blind eye on God's commandments while participating in the routine activities of our lives. As long as everyone else is doing it we somehow feel justified in our sinful behavior.

Conform to God, Not the World

We claim to be Christian but why aren't we acting like one? I think one of the biggest mistakes we make is to compare our behavior to the world around us. How we are perceived by others, whether or not they are Christian, is very important to us and sometimes we find ourselves compromising our values to gain this acceptance. The world offers us guidelines that have been accumulated throughout history. This wealth of knowledge fills our libraries, schools, government, and the minds of all of us. As Christians, we must rely on God's wisdom to try and make sense of all this information and determine what is right and wrong. (Romans 12:2)

> *Do not conform any longer to the pattern of this world, but be transformed by the renewing of your mind. Then you will be able to test and approve what God's will is—his good, pleasing and perfect will.*

God knew how confusing it would be so He gave us a road map explaining in perfect detail how to live holy lives. The Bible is far more than just a road map; this brilliant book enriches us with God's living Word and contains more information than we would ever need to live Christian lives. If we truly followed all of God's commandments with love and obedience, this world would be a much better place.

Unfortunately, the world has decided to ignore God and has written its own version of the commandments. In today's generation, it appears that the worldly version is winning and the consequences have been devastating. As Christians, why do we compromise and follow the world's standards when we have the true Word of God? The pressure to be worldly is intense and not even the strongest Christian is immune to it. But is being accepted by society worth jeopardizing our relationship with our Heavenly Father? And why does the world reject us when we follow God's ways? (John 15:19)

> *If the world hates you, keep in mind that it hated me first. If you belonged to the world, it would love you as its own. As it is, you do not belong to the world, but I have chosen you out of the world. That is why the world hates you. Remember the words I spoke to you: 'No servant is greater than his master.' 'If they persecuted me, they will persecute you also. If they obeyed my teaching, they will obey yours also . . . .'*

No one likes to be called a fanatic so we try and do a balancing act. On one hand, we compromise our faith to fit in with society, on the other, we try and satisfy God. This is a mistake and Scripture is clear that serving God must be our first priority. (Romans 12:1,2)

> *Therefore, I urge you, brothers, in view of God's mercy, to offer your bodies as living sacrifices, holy and pleasing to God—this is your spiritual act of worship. Do not conform any longer to the pattern of this world, but be transformed by the renewing of your mind. Then you will be able to test and approve what God's will is—his good, pleasing and perfect will.*

Despite these words from our Lord, we continue to make it a high priority to be accepted by others and spend millions of dollars and countless hours of our time trying to fit in. We even go so far as to be ashamed of Jesus when in the presence of secular people. How many times have we been with a group of friends outside the protected walls of the church either at work or at play, and someone rips off the Lord's name in vain, or they make a crass joke that belittles our faith, or they start gossiping about someone we know and we just sit there silent.

I learned first hand what it was like to be embarrassed of Jesus back in the eighth grade. My brother was sitting alone at a study hall desk drawing on his notebook cover. I was standing at a distance and noticed several kids had come up and started talking to him. It didn't look friendly so I went over to see what was going on. Close up, it was apparent that the kids were making fun of him for writing Jesus in large block letters that was clearly visible to anyone walking by. He just sat there taking the abuse and continued with his drawing. My body froze up and I didn't say a word in my brother's defense. Instead, tantalizing fear and embarrassment paralyzed me – not only did I abandon my brother who courageously stood his ground, I rejected Jesus by being ashamed of his name. Being associated with Jesus was not socially accepted back then just as it isn't today. All I could think about was the Scripture that referred to people like me. (Mark 8:38)

> *If anyone is ashamed of me and my words in this adulterous and sinful generation, the Son of Man will be ashamed of him when he comes in his Father's glory with the holy angels.*

Because of the huge gap between secularism and Christianity in our generation, living a Christian life is no simple task. That is why it is so easy to be labeled a fanatic. I realize that fanaticism can be a dangerous thing and has caused many problems throughout our world, but we have to be careful not to be intimidated when given this name just for peacefully living out our faith. The key word here is "peacefully." Some distort our faith by using it as a means to pursue their own warped desires. I'm talking about living a true Christian life, one where we are faithful to our Lord without watering down His Word. (John 15:9-13)

> *As the Father has loved me, so have I loved you. Now remain in my love. If you obey my commands, you will remain in my love, just as I have obeyed my Father's commands and remain in his love. I have told you this so that my joy may be in you and that your joy may be complete. My command is this: Love each other as I have loved you. Greater love has no one than this, that he lay down his life for his friends.*

Unfortunately, society has removed itself from Godly principles and will only accept Christians who will conform to their worldly values. In other words, if the world completely accepts us, we must be doing something wrong – that is how bad things have become. It probably won't get better any time soon because the world has no foundation in which to build moral principles essential for society to peacefully co-exist. The longer the world chooses to go without God, the more evil it will become. The breakdown of society is right before our eyes and it appears that even the Earth and some of its natural cycles are changing for the worse.

We are living in a critical period of time. Our world is in desperate need of God and it is our responsibility as Christians to share His love with others around us through our word and by example. If we don't, who will?

Our country was founded on Godly principles by men and women who understood their importance and many of them were willing to give up their fortunes and even their lives for this noble cause. It's unfortunate that we have chipped away at these hard fought principles and are presently at risk of losing some of them.

Looking back, it is amazing how young our country really is. All we have to do is talk to our grandparents and hear their stories to realize the American journey has really just begun. Only a relatively short time ago, there were no TVs or other electronic devices we now take for granted. For some of them, cars were not even available and if they were, most people back then couldn't afford one. It is amazing to see how far and fast we have come technologically as a nation in such a relatively short period of time. However, we are at best a teenager compared to the age of other countries. Like a teenager, we are fearless, full of ambition, willing to take risks, extremely competitive, and insatiably independent. At the same time we are passionate, loving, generous, and dedicated to upholding the values we believe in. We are liberators of truth, justice, and freedom for all. Because of this, the United States has been blessed by God like no other nation in history. However, like a teenager, we sometimes get a little rebellious and think we know more than we really do. Sometimes we also don't know when to stop ourselves even if it gets us into trouble. It is disheartening for me and others to see our nation, so full of potential, deviating from the very source of our greatness. We have to pray that we will come back to the God-given values on which our country was founded.

If we are serious about this, we have to start living like a true Christian. In order to be successful, we have to quit using the world as the standard to determine how good or bad we are. The comment, "We're better than most," doesn't cut it. Our values did not come from the world, but rather, from God who is perfect and all knowing. Why then do we continue to challenge his authority by coming up with our own modified version of His commandments? If we were talking about a secular person, this behavior would be understandable, but we are Christian and have no excuse to rationalize our disobedient behavior. Becoming a true Christian carries with it responsibilities that can only be realized through faithful commitment and prayer.

Forms of Unbelief

The secular world is working hard to win the minds of all of us and as a result, we have become overwhelmed with distractions that succeed in taking our time away from God and our families. Belief in God has become more difficult because we do not spend enough time in prayer with Him. Most of us say we believe, but our actions sometimes tell a different story. It is not enough to just believe in God, even the devil does that much. We have to back up our belief with love, and if we truly love God, we will follow His commandments and serve Him. In other words, we need to act like a true Christian, not just proclaim to be one.

Fear and anxiety are forms of unbelief that cause us to deny Christ's ability to help when it goes beyond our own ability to solve a problem. Unbelief has many forms and the only way to overcome this obstacle is to put our trust in God, not in ourselves. He is the master problem solver and to put our trust in anything less can cause paralyzing fear and despair.

Despite all the challenges we face, most of us believe there is a God, so if we believe, what are we doing about it? Do we act any different than the secular people around us? In today's society, the spirit of antichrist is everywhere and it has become difficult to live out our Christian faith without being ridiculed or labeled a fanatic by the secular world and even by some Christians. This has caused some of us to live two lives – we act Christian when around Christians and act secular when around the secular to avoid any conflicts. Because of this, Christian principles have been infected with secular ideologies which have caused some of us to water down our faith and become lukewarm. (Revelation 3:16)

> I know your deeds, that you are neither cold nor hot.
> I wish you were either one or the other! So, because
> you are lukewarm—neither hot nor cold—I am
> about to spit you out of my mouth.

Media/Entertainment

Probably one of the strongest influences in our lives is the media. There are countless forms of information and entertainment available at the click of a button through television, radio, DVDs, other electronic devices, movie theaters, and of course through the Internet. In the secular media, God is rarely mentioned, and if He is, it is out of disrespect. How many times have we watched a movie where our Creator's name has been taken in vain? This should make us squirm in our seats, but unfortunately, some of us continue watching and hardly even notice. We have been inundated with this type of language which has numbed our senses.

Sex, violence, anti-family, anti-Christian scenes constantly flash before our eyes, over and over, day after day. For most of us, this has been going on since our youth and will continue into old age. Why have we become so comfortable with this type of sin? Have our consciences become paralyzed and our standards stripped away? What form of rationalization has allowed us to justify watching this type of immoral behavior? How can we sit there with our families and expose them to this type of material, especially with our children present? I don't think most of us do this intentionally;

rather, we do it out of blind ignorance and have become a victim of a "frog in boiling water." Little by little, the entertainment industry has exposed us to this and over time, the standards we once held have been eroded away.

We are now seeing things on public television that would have shocked us only a decade ago. Though it may have partially resulted from our ignorance, it still doesn't dismiss us from this sin. If we are watching a movie and didn't know before hand that the Lord's name would be taken in vain, there would be no sin. However, if we continue to watch the movie regardless, we have violated our Lord's commandment. In good conscience, how can we hear blasphemy against our Creator and continue watching? Furthermore, how could any movie be good enough to allow us to sin against God? Some might say, "It's just an example of real life" or "It was the only swear word in the whole show and the rest of it was really clean." Breaking any of the Commandments can never be justified – Christians have a higher standard to follow.

I've been in that situation before where I continued watching a movie I was really into despite hearing God's name taken in vain. It was a good show and my family was really enjoying it – good moral lessons were being taught and all seemed well until out of the blue, God's name was taken in vain. We all instantly looked at each other and wanted to ignore what had happened. I broke the silence and yelled out, "Why did they have to say that?" That night, however, I compromised our faith by not turning it off. Instead, we continued watching the movie and knowingly sinned against our Lord. (Exodus 20:7)

> *You shall not misuse the name of the LORD your God, for the LORD will not hold anyone guiltless who misuses his name.*

By becoming a willing participant, I was guilty of blaspheming His holy name. I felt ashamed and made a sincere commitment to not allow it to happen again. The next time it occurred, God gave me the strength to turn it off. I took it back to the video store and explained the problem and they were more than happy to refund my money and even apologized for the inconvenience.

Music/Television

As a Christian, how can we justify watching and/or listening to anything that includes pornography (blatant or subtle), foul language, extreme violence that has no just cause, or anything else that is contrary to our faith? What about the commercials that quickly flash sex scenes in front of our children's eyes before we can do anything about it? I feel that these types of commercials present one of the most dangerous threats to our kids. Unless our televisions are monitored closely, they are at risk of being exposed to graphic scenes used by the networks to draw interest to their latest programs. These images can stick in their minds for a lifetime and can replay over and over again. The damage from this can be devastating and as responsible parents, we must do everything possible to prevent this from occurring.

It would probably be better to ban television all together and replace it with approved videos but this option isn't always practical. Muting the commercials and telling our children to turn their heads may work if we're in the room with them, but this demands a lot of discipline by both the parent and the child. This technique used to give our son a sore neck from having to turn his head so often. Using technology to completely block commercials is the best way but may not be available to everyone. We finally got tired of regular TV and switched to a family friendly satellite option instead. Even some of these programs have to be monitored. That is why password protected parental locks should always be used.

One minute we're telling our children not to do immoral things and the next, we're allowing them to watch and listen to it on TV and other electronic devices. This is a conflict of interest detrimental to our children's wellbeing. God specifically condemns any act that causes harm to a child. (Matthew 18:6)

> *But if anyone causes one of these little ones who believe in me to sin, it would be better for him to have a large millstone hung around his neck and to be drowned in the depths of the sea.*

My wife and I had the opportunity to see a large millstone first hand while visiting Israel. It must have weighed over 500 pounds. I don't think anyone would like a millstone tied around their neck but that is exactly what will happen to us (not literally but something even worse) if we continue to allow our children to participate in unGodly material.

There is no excuse or rationalization that will justify us exposing our children (or ourselves for that matter) to this filth. Some of us are proud to tell others that we don't allow our kids to watch bad shows but feel comfortable watching it ourselves. What kind of message is that sending – that it's ok to watch this garbage as long as we're an adult? Isn't it a sin no matter what age we are? We need to wake up as Christians and start setting a proper example by not participating in any form of entertainment that is contrary to God's Word.

Internet

The Internet has become one of the largest assets and threats to nearly everyone in society. Never before has information been so readily available. If used properly, it can change our lives in a positive way. Conversely, misusing it can lead to utter destruction.

Children and young adults are vulnerable to child predators and other hazards that are constantly lurking online. Parents should always monitor their children while they're online and should install the proper parental controls necessary to keep track of their activity. A reliable firewall and popup blocker along with a quality anti-virus and content monitoring program are essential tools to help combat this onslaught from the enemy. Failure to do this can result in unwanted material such as pornographic images being displayed directly in front of children and adults. Addiction to pornography has and continues to destroy anyone affected by it – Christians are not immune.

In my opinion, the only way we can overcome this crisis is through prayer and fasting. We cannot handle this on our own – we need God's power to break this satanic vice that holds some of us and our families in spiritual and physical bondage. Being accountable to God is the only way to avoid evil things. We have to be strict in this area even if we're not popular with our children, their friends, and even our own friends.

Even if the material being viewed is not offensive, we still have a responsibility as parents to set reasonable boundaries on how much time our children spend on electronic devices. Addictions to things such as texting, video games, social networks, and other electronic media have become a real problem in our present times and it is up to parents to help keep this in proper perspective. As Christians, we are not here for a popularity contest; rather, we are here to serve our Lord. Through our obedience, we allow Christ's precious blood to protect us which enables our families to receive the type of true joy the world cannot give us. (Joshua 24:15)

> "... But as for me and my household, we will serve the LORD."

Clothing

What about the little things we do on a daily basis that can compromise our Christian faith. How we present ourselves by the way we dress can have a tremendous impact, either positive or negative, in our walk with Christ.

Inappropriate dress can lead the best of Christians into temptation which can further lead to the sin of lust and even adultery. If a woman or a man dresses in such a way that causes another to lust after them, the person causing the other to sin may be just as guilty. (Matthew 5:27,28), (Luke 17:1), (Romans 14:13)

> *You have heard that it was said, 'Do not commit adultery.' I tell you that anyone who looks at a woman lustfully has already committed adultery with her in his heart.*

> *Jesus said to his disciples: "Things that cause people to sin are bound to come, but woe to that person through whom they come.*

> *Therefore let us stop passing judgment on one another. Instead, make up your mind not to put any stumbling block or obstacle in your brother's way.*

As Christians, we have an extra responsibility to be consciously aware of how we dress and how we present ourselves in society. After all, our bodies do not belong to us but are the temple of the Holy Spirit. Showing respect to God, ourselves, and others around us is far more important than conforming to our culture. We cannot allow ourselves to feel justified just because everyone else is doing it.

There is nothing wrong with wearing something popular as long as it appropriately covers our body. If our clothing or lack thereof is causing others to lust, we are probably dressed too revealing. Of course there are always those who will lust no matter what we wear even if we are dressed appropriately. Obviously, there is no sin on our part in that situation. Let's face it, God has made man and woman a beautiful sight to behold and therefore, we are naturally attracted to the opposite sex. But as Christians, we have to keep our emotions under control and save the lion share of this attraction for our current or future spouse. Wearing clothes a little looser and less revealing without highlighting every bodily detail can go a long way in preventing others from getting the wrong idea. In turn, we will be more pleasing to Christ and will gain more respect from those around us. I know this topic may cause some controversy and will appear to be outdated, but we cannot forget that God's Word never gets old. (1 Timothy 2:9), (1 Peter 3:3-5)

> *I also want women to dress modestly, with decency and propriety, not with braided hair or gold or pearls or expensive clothes, but with good deeds, appropriate for women who profess to worship God.*
>
> *Your beauty should not come from outward adornment, such as braided hair and the wearing of gold jewelry and fine clothes. Instead, it should be that of your inner self, the unfading beauty of a gentle and quiet spirit, which is of great worth in God's sight. For this is the way the holy women of the past who put their hope in God used to make themselves beautiful.*

Swearing

What comes out of our mouths makes a public statement and can determine what level of respect others will have towards us. In our present times, four-letter words have been integrated into all levels of society and are freely spoken at work and in other areas that were once off limits to this type of talk. When Christians are exposed to foul language day in and day out, we can become immune to its rudeness and before long, we find ourselves talking like secular people around us. This type of talk isn't limited to construction sites and is widely used in the white collar professions and has even infected the church.

While out in public, it is easy to hear these words used on a regular basis but the one that troubles me the most is when our Lord's name is taken in vain. If I hear someone say it around me, I sometimes ask them why they are cursing God. In return, I usually just get a blank stare or they say, "I wasn't cursing God, it's just an expression." For most of us, I believe we are not intentionally blaspheming God but have just picked up a horrible habit. This still does not relieve us from this sin and what a sin it is! This type of language is understandable coming from a non-believer, but for a Christian, it is completely unacceptable and is a direct violation of God's commandments. We have to be careful what comes out of our mouth especially when it blasphemes our Lord.

We are using God's name in vain whenever we mention it in a disrespectful manner. If we use the phrase, "Oh my God" or "God," unless we are referring to Him in a sincere manner, we may be guilty of using His name in vain. This is a very serious problem and should not be taken lightly. We should never forget who we are dealing with. (Revelation 1:8)

> "I am the Alpha and the Omega," says the Lord God, "who is, and who was, and who is to come, the Almighty."

This topic reminds me of a tile setter who did a small job for me on a bathroom remodel. He could not speak one sentence without most of the known swear words being used which included taking our Lord's name in vain. I told him to quit swearing especially in front of my client and he responded by laughing hysterically. I repeated myself and this time he knew I was serious, so he agreed to make a deal with me. He paused for a moment as if in deep thought and then quickly blurted out every swear word in the book, with the exception of the Lord's name taken in vain. He then exclaimed, "How's that?" He started laughing wildly again. I realized at that moment, this was the only vocabulary he understood. I replied, "Good enough if that's all you can manage." He knew how much I hated to hear God's name taken in vain so he stayed true to his word by not saying it throughout the rest of the project. Deep down, he is a good guy, but for whatever reason, developed the worst swearing habit imaginable.

Swearing can be very addictive and habit-forming especially when we get angry. I know, because I used to swear on a regular basis until God delivered me from this sin through many hours of prayer and fasting. It's kind of a funny thing when someone comes up to me in casual conversation and starts cussing up a storm and then they suddenly realize that I'm not swearing. They stop and sometimes apologize for doing it. I have found when people know I don't cuss very often, they usually keep it clean around me. Misery loves company and without company some of us feel embarrassed and a little convicted when swearing around other people who don't. On the other hand, if we get into a group where one person starts up, it can catch on like wildfire. Once the cussing starts, the other person holding back joins in. If we participate in this type of behavior, we are no longer a witness for Christ, but rather, have joined the ranks of the secular world.

I still struggle holding back the "S" and other words on occasions, especially when angry or excited about something. However, there is no excuse for this behavior. No matter what the situation or how much peer pressure is placed upon us, we have to clean up our mouths in order to follow Christ and become the example he wants us to be. This is clearly stated in the following Scripture. (Ephesians 4:29)

> *Do not let any unwholesome talk come out of your mouths, but only what is helpful for building others up according to their needs, that it may benefit those who listen.*

Lying

There is nothing worse than a liar, yet most of us have committed this sin one time or another. There are hundreds of excuses to justify a lie but none of them are worthy of the truth. Some lies are more obvious that get us into trouble while others are more subtle that often go unnoticed, at least temporarily. In my opinion, it is the "white lies" that cause the most problems because they are easier for us to rationalize.

I recently caught my son telling a lie and disciplined him by taking away his cell phone. I was pretty hard on him but I wanted to make an example out of it. For the most part, he has been truthful with us and we didn't want this to escalate into a pattern. In my adolescent years, there was a period in my life when I became addicted to lying to get what I wanted or to get out of trouble.

When I was around eight, I attended a youth Christian camp which was located on the edge of a medium-sized lake tucked away at the base of a beautiful mountain peak. When we were loading the bus to return home, our group leader caught me shoving frogs into my pockets. He was mean natured and I remember being terrified when he grabbed my arm and asked what I was hiding in my pockets. "Nothing," I replied. He then shook me and demanded I take the frogs out. I went over to edge of the lake and pretended to release them. Instead, I placed them under the front of my shirt and tucked it in. I had at least three or four frogs crawling on my body as I entered the bus for the two-hour journey home.

Shortly after departing, I fell asleep and was awakened by kids yelling and screaming as the frogs had escaped and were jumping all over the floor of the bus. When the mean group leader found out I had disobeyed him, I thought I was dead! Again, I lied to him when he angrily asked me if I had done this. I replied, "No sir, someone else must have brought them aboard." For whatever reason, the leader didn't like me from the start and he wasn't about to let me off the hook. Instead, he used it as an opportunity to yell at me for the next several miles to vent off some steam. I seriously thought this guy was going to physically hurt me. Even though my lie didn't get me out of trouble, I continued doing it off and on for a few more years whenever I found myself in trouble.

Thank goodness I out grew this sin, or at least I thought I had. A little while after disciplining my son for his lie, he busted me while playing golf. On a downhill tee I hit a horrible shot that traveled less than one-hundred yards. I then hit another ball that had good distance but appeared to go out of bounds into a bordering homeowner's yard. As we were walking down the hill, a golfer walked in front of us to try and find his miss-hit ball from the adjacent fairway. I then reached down to pick up my poorly hit ball and the golfer just stared at me. With a grin on his face and in a cocky tone he replied, "Why didn't ya hit that ball, what's wrong with it?" He knew darn well that it was a bad shot so I gave into his cynicism and quickly ripped off a lie by replying, "That was just a practice ball I hit with my pitching wedge, the ball I'm playing is way down there." Part of me was just joking (who would use a pitching wedge on a par 4 tee shot?) but another part was trying to save face.

I didn't even think about it afterwards until my son who was listening, later chewed me out for telling the lie. And boy did he rub it in! This was his moment to get back at me and get back at me he did. He also helped awaken me to the fact that I had been telling these types of lies more frequently than I would like to admit. The fact that I am usually honest and do not tell big lies doesn't lessen the severity of the smaller "white lies." It was now staring me right in the face with no way to rationalize it. God used my son to help expose my sin. At first I was angry with him for exposing the truth, but later after thinking it over, I realized I was fortunate to have this out in the open. I asked Jesus to forgive me and told Him I would make a sincere effort to not let it happen again. It is always a good thing when sin is purged out of our lives.

That night, I stayed up late watching a good movie about the Apostle Paul's life so I slept in the next morning. Without notice, a friend came over around 9:00 a.m. I had just gotten into the shower when he arrived. My wife came in and told me to come out right away. I was embarrassed to be caught at home this late on a work day so my mind started to quickly come up with an excuse to save myself from embarrassment. I was just about to come up with an excuse when I remembered what had happened the day before. Instead, I didn't say anything but felt extremely uncomfortable trapped in my predicament. I acted as if I was up for hours which was misleading by action. I finally gave up the act and told him I stayed up late watching a movie and had a hard time waking up. After saying this, I felt relieved and wondered why I didn't just say it to begin with. My friend hadn't come over for a while which led me to believe that his arrival wasn't a coincidence. God was testing me and I nearly blew it just after telling Him I would make an effort to eliminate my convenient lies.

All lies, whether they are large or small are wrong. However, there are a few obvious exceptions. An example would be to help prevent you or someone else from being harmed or to tell someone they look nice when you really think they look awful. Regardless, lying is responsible for destroying everything it affects including marriages, families, relationships, businesses, governments, and even entire nations.

† † †

It can seem overwhelming to truly follow God's Word. That is why it is important for Christians to always have Jesus on our minds and hearts – He will strengthen and convict us if we are about to sin. When we fail to spend time in prayer, we become more vulnerable to temptation. In other words, it is only through Christ that we can avoid sin in the literal and spiritual sense. The Scriptures below remind us that our sins will not go unnoticed and will cause us to give an account to our Lord. However, if we ask Jesus to forgive us with a repentant heart, He will always be there to cover our transgressions with his precious blood. He will also steer us back to the path of righteousness where we belong. (Proverbs 10:9), (Hebrew 4:13), (1 John 2:1-6)

> *The man of integrity walks securely, but he who takes crooked paths will be found out.*

Nothing in all creation is hidden from God's sight. Everything is uncovered and laid bare before the eyes of Him to whom we must give account.

My dear children, I write this to you so that you will not sin. But if anybody does sin, we have one who speaks to the Father in our defense—Jesus Christ, the Righteous One. He is the atoning sacrifice for our sins, and not only for ours but also for the sins of the whole world.

We know that we have come to know him if we obey his commands. The man who says, "I know him," but does not do what he commands is a liar, and the truth is not in him. But if anyone obeys his word, God's love is truly made complete in him. This is how we know we are in him: Whoever claims to live in him must walk as Jesus did.

Because he loves us, God will expose our lies just as he used my son to expose mine. I pray I will learn the lesson that no matter how insignificant it may appear, lying never pays off but only separates us from Christ.

God wants us to live a long productive life building up His kingdom. Therefore, anything that causes harm to us or others around us must be avoided at all times. Whether we're praying, coaching a little league baseball team, raising a family, on a date, attending class, at work, at play . . . , we must never forget who we are and what example we are trying to portray because the world is watching our every move with desperate eyes, searching for the truth that only God can give.

Chapter 2

Christian Responsibilities

Unequally Yoked

It can be much easier to live a Christian life if we surround ourselves with others who have the same belief. I am not saying that we should abandon our ministry to unbelievers; rather, we have to be careful when hanging around secular people to avoid compromising our faith in order to please them. God wants us to help them, not become like them. This is especially true when dealing with relationships. Whether it's with a best friend or our future spouse, Scripture has warned us that it is best to remain equally yoked. (2 Corinthians 6:14,15,17)

> *Do not be yoked together with unbelievers. For what do righteousness and wickedness have in common? Or what fellowship can light have with darkness?*
>
> *What does a believer have in common with an unbeliever?*
>
> *"Therefore come out from them and be separate, says the Lord. Touch no unclean thing, and I will receive you."*

It is important to note that in the context of this Scripture, the Apostle Paul was speaking to a society who heavily worshiped idols. However, this doesn't mean it's not relevant today. Some Christians are strong enough in their faith to endure being unequally yoked but others are not which can lead to many problems if they do not follow Christ's advice. This doesn't mean we shouldn't associate with anyone who doesn't believe; instead, we have to be careful to not let them influence our faith in the wrong direction, no matter how much we like or respect them. It also doesn't mean that all unbelievers are evil. Like many others, I have personally met secular people who act more Christian-like than some Christians do. Regardless, it is better for Christians to yoke with Christians because this allows us to better share our faith in Christ.

Mom and Dad

Like with the rest of us, my dad who has since passed away, had his good and bad qualities. He was polite, never interrupted people while they were talking, rarely cursed, a genius in mathematics, an extremely hard worker, and an excellent provider for our family. His weakness was his inability to control his drinking and smoking habits which later cost him his life.

My mom and dad married at a very young age and were definitely unequally yoked. Mom was like most teenagers who thought she knew better. She went ahead and got married knowing that my dad already had a drinking problem and didn't practice his faith in God. Her decision was ironic because she already knew first hand the pain of living with an alcoholic because her dad suffered from this disease. When Grandpa was first introduced to my dad, he warned my mom to stay away from him because he had already run into him on several occasion at the local bar. The last thing he wanted for his daughter was another potential alcoholic like himself.

Mom didn't listen to her dad's advice and on their wedding day during the reception, a few of my dad's friends grabbed him and threw him into the back of their 57 Chevy, took off, and didn't return for several hours. All alone, Mom sat outside on the church stairs probably wondering for the first time what she had gotten herself into. Their story was the classic tale of the innocent girl who runs off with a "James Dean" type character and boy did my dad fit Dean's image to a "t." Mom's decision led her and the rest of our family through some good and bad times, and by the grace of God, they stayed married until death took them apart.

Dad was born in 1944 in a small mountain town that relied heavily on the logging industry. He had two sisters who were over ten years older than him who had already left home so he grew up as an only child. When he was a teenager, his parents decided to move to the Desert Southwest to open up a trading post. My dad refused to go with them so his older sister and brother-in-law offered to look after him so he could finish his high school years in his hometown. This was a generous offer considering they already had four kids of their own to take care of when money was tight. My dad developed a close relationship with their family and later with my mom which is why I am here today to tell their story. It is amazing how the decisions we make in life change the course of our own history and those around us.

Though my dad was quite the rebel, he balanced it out with a responsible side. He graduated from college with a math degree and continued on with his education to become a civil engineer. He did all this while holding down a full time job and two kids already under his belt. My brother was the firstborn and I came less than a year later. When I was first introduced to my older brother, he smashed a glass ashtray over my head. I guess that was just his way to let me know who was boss. Later when my sister was born, my parents brought her home with two shiny red fire trucks – no ashtray on the head for her.

After finishing college, Dad landed a job with a large construction company who specialized in road and bridge work. He found himself helping with the structural design of a large cloverleaf overpass which included estimating the time required, from start to finish, to complete the project. After a successful short career working for someone else, he decided to go off and form his own company. This meant giving up benefits and a steady paycheck but he was an entrepreneur at heart and nothing was going to stop him from achieving his goals. I always respected Dad for his courage to go it alone. He taught my brother and me the valuable lesson of hard work which gave us the confidence to later form our own companies.

Dad claimed to have a belief in God but did not openly practice his faith. This caused strain on their marriage because my mom could never share her faith with him, resulting in a lonely spiritual life. Our family made it a priority to constantly pray for Dad, but to be honest, I had a hard time believing he would ever come to our Lord in an open way. Don't get me wrong, I love my dad and wouldn't have traded him for anyone but our relationship was not complete because God was not included in it. We especially enjoyed hunting and fishing together and this became our common bond.

Dad was emotional inside but rarely outwardly expressed it –we never hugged or exchanged "I love you's." His parents, especially his mom, were stoic in nature and my dad took after them. His dad died when I was young; therefore, I didn't spend enough time with Grandpa in order to develop a relationship. It wasn't until my mid- twenties that I developed a good relationship with my grandma whom I visited on a regular basis. She was instrumental in setting up our family reunions which kept my dad's side of the family better connected.

Grandpa

I was fortunate to have a grandpa on my mom's side of the family who helped show me the emotional and spiritual side of life that my dad wasn't able to give. I was barely old enough to remember when Grandpa had his drinking problem. On one occasion, I vaguely remember lying awake in bed at my grandparents' house when I heard a loud crashing sound of glass breaking outside my open window. Grandpa had come home after being at the bar and decided to throw his empty wine bottle on the brick-paved sidewalk before entering the house. Grandma was waiting up for him and also heard the noise. She met him at the door and an argument ensued that caused my little three-year-old stomach to become tied into knots. By the grace of God, Grandpa miraculously recovered from his alcohol problem several years later. It didn't happen exactly the way he intended but in the end, he was healed.

Desperately praying in an empty church while drunk, he pleaded with God to heal him from his alcohol problem. God didn't deliver him from alcohol that day, but instead he was instantly delivered from his addiction to smoking. From that day forward, Grandpa never had the desire to smoke again. God in His wisdom knew that if he quit smoking, the drinking would follow and that's exactly what happened soon afterwards. With the bondage of smoking and drinking gone, he became the person God had intended all along – a wonderful spiritual leader for our family and a powerful prayer warrior, not only for us, but for others around him. His Irish temper would still get the best of him which gave him the nickname, "The Wild Man," but he had a tender side to him that could melt the hardest of hearts.

Grandpa was born in 1913 at the tail end of the Industrial Revolution. He was one of five children (three brothers and one sister) born in a small mining town in the rugged mountains of the Southwest. He grew up in a town that still had the character of the Wild West. In addition to a few cars, people still used horse and buggy to get around on the muddy pothole and rut-laden dirt streets. Even though mining had long since reached its peak and was winding down, the town was still pretty hardcore with all its saloons and other activities typically found in the mining era.

Grandpa told me a story about a hanging that took place near his home. He said it was so gruesome to watch that it almost made him lose his lunch. He claimed that hangings were rare in public at that time and hoped to never witness another one.

I then asked him if he had ever witnessed a gunfight. He was quick to tell me that the movies showing expert dead-on shots from gunslingers was a myth for most people back then. He went on to tell me about the one and only gunfight he had witnessed. According to Grandpa, two men got into a scuffle over an accusation that the other man had stolen his horse. The man accused, challenged the other to a gunfight. Grandpa said that people cleared the street just like in the movies but when the first shots were fired, both men lay on the ground wounded, one hit in the arm and the other in the leg. However, this didn't stop them and they continued shooting at each other with most shots from both sides missing their targets. Before it was all over, each man had emptied their pistols but had only been lucky enough to hit the other's extremities. Even though neither of them had been fatally shot, they both ended up bleeding to death from their wounds. Grandpa said this was typical in gunfights because most of them were such a bad shot which is contrary to what the movies portray.

† † †

Grandpa's youngest brother was confined to a wheelchair most of his life so Grandpa took him under his wing which resulted in a close, symbiotic relationship. His handicapped brother was more level headed and never developed a drinking problem and was loved by most all who came in contact with him. This allowed him to help Grandpa personally with his problems and smooth out their joint business ventures.

They started up one of the first Packard Jeep dealerships in their region. The income from the business helped support not only Grandpa's immediate family and his brother, but also his other siblings. It became a family partnership which still survives today. Grandpa was always very generous with his time and money and helped family and strangers on a regular basis. He and Grandma had four children (three sons and a daughter).

On one occasion, Grandpa was searching for a piece of property for their Packard dealership when he noticed a young boy outside without shoes on in the middle of the winter. Grandpa was a deal maker so he told God that he would buy the boy some shoes if He would help him find a good deal on some real estate. On the same day he bought the boy some shoes, a man offered to sell him a piece of real estate that was divided in two by a railroad track. He thought about it and came up with the idea of obtaining an option to buy with the intent to sell the other half divided by the tracks to another party. The man accepted his offer and within a short period of time, Grandpa was able to sell the other half of the property for the same price he bought the entire lot for. In other words, he ended up getting the property for free. Grandpa and his brother knew this was from God and they dedicated their shop to the Lord.

Great Grandpa

Grandpa's father was heavily into mining and was the foreman at several prominent gold and silver mines and prospected on his own as well. According to Grandpa, his dad was tough as nails. He was short in stature but made up for it with grit. He never looked for trouble, but when it came his way, look out! He was likened to a wolverine when defending himself, friends, co-workers, or his family. Men much taller than him would cower when he became angry. Grandpa said his dad was honest, well respected, and an extremely hard worker. He had a special talent for finding gold and had several major finds attributed to his skills.

Great Grandpa's largest find while working for himself occurred at the Neglected Mine located in the mountains of Southwest Colorado. He discovered an extremely rich vein of gold there and recruited four partners to help finance the large operation. He had finally found his "mother lode." Feeling optimistic about his financial future, he decided to get married late in life. Everything seemed to be going well. He and his partners had a large crew of men working for them and the rich vein discovered turned out to be a very profitable grade of telluride ore which contained a high content of gold with some silver mixed in.

Word of their success quickly spread around the area and according to Grandpa, shortly afterward a company offered them

$1 million for the rights to their mine. Great Grandpa was ready to jump on the offer but the other partners couldn't let go of the rich gold, so by unanimous vote the offer was rejected. He did everything he could to talk them into it but to no avail. His experience had taught him that mining was unpredictable and could change as fast as the weather.

After Great Grandpa had been away for a time to manage another mine in the central part of the state, one of his partners high-graded a fair amount of the rich gold, disappeared, never to be seen again. It was rumored that he fled to England and entertained royalty with his new found fortune and later went broke with nothing to show for it. Shortly afterwards, their mine abruptly ran out of gold which marked the end of the road for them at this particular claim.

I'm sure that Great Grandpa and the other partners looked back many times in their lives, wishing they had taken the generous offer when they had the chance. Just like with many of us today, we find ourselves in the same situation, looking back wishing we had made a different decision. Regardless, the mine became famous in the Southwest and is still recognized today.

† † †

Grandpa carried on his father's tradition and later purchased several mining claims of his own. The acquisition of one of his claims was a dream come true. Great Grandpa told him a story where he came across some drunken miners who were going around town bragging about a rich find they had recently discovered. Being a self-taught expert, Great Grandpa asked if he could examine a sample of their gold. He claimed it was one of the richer samples he'd seen.

Years later, Grandpa's father told him if he ever had a chance to purchase the claim where the rich gold came from, to jump on it. Great Grandpa believed there was still more gold to be found and Grandpa believed him with all of his heart. When it finally came up for sale years later, he jumped on it.

Thanks to Grandpa, our family still owns this beautiful mining claim located high in the Rocky Mountains. It is nestled in a post- glacial bowl, surrounded on three sides by towering peaks well above timberline. Today, we use it more as a camping and hiking destination to enjoy the beautiful scenery than we do as a goldmine.

Frightened Campers at the Mine

When I was around eight years old, my mom and grandma took us camping to this site which proved to be a memorable experience. It took an hour to drive up to the base of the peak where the mine was located and another hour to slowly wind up the rough four-wheel-drive road leading to our destination. Back in the 1950's, Grandpa, with the help of his son and an experienced bull dozer operator, built the road to his mining claim. Grandpa's main job was to set off the dynamite to help clear off areas too rocky for the bulldozer to blade through. As they slowly made progress up the steep terrain, he followed behind with an old school bus that was later converted into a mining camp.

Our family also used the old aluminum bus for a camper and this is where we would set up camp after arriving. About three-quarters of the way up the mountain, the road flattens out into a park just below timberline. It was there that I remember spotting a magnificent six-point bull elk feeding in the thick brush along a stream bed. That got me all pumped up and I couldn't wait to get out of the truck to explore the vast wilderness that surrounded us.

It was late afternoon when we arrived and by the time we unloaded everything and set up camp, there was only enough daylight to take a short hike up the beautifully manicured alpine slope before nightfall. My brother and sister and I hiked up to a point that overlooked the alpine meadow where we were camped. The sun had just set but the awesome mountain peaks that jutted up on three sides of us were still clearly visible. Down below, we could see our camp nestled between some willows with a small brook gently winding back and forth along the valley floor.

While taking in the beautiful scenery, we were suddenly interrupted by a loud growling noise off in the distance. With fear in our eyes, we just looked at one another. We had taken our uncle's dog, Coronado, with us and he was also looking intently in the direction of the noise. Without saying a word, we took off running down the hill to the safety of the camp. We had heard stories of large bears that roamed these parts and weren't about to take any chances. Rushing into the old bus out of breath, we told Mom and Grandma of our encounter and they told us it was probably just a stray sheep that was common in the summertime.

This didn't make me feel any better when I had to use the outhouse later that night. As soon as I stepped outside of the bus into the pitch black night, my heart nearly pounded out of my chest. Coronado, a German shepherd lab mix, came out with me and immediately started barking in a certain direction acting like he saw something off in the distance. This made me even more afraid so I quickly did my duty and hurried back into the safety of the bus. There was an old wood burning stove used for heating and cooking located directly up the steps at the entrance of the bus. I came running in so fast that I failed to yield before turning the corner and slammed into the side of the stove, severely burning my arm. That wasn't the worst of it.

After dressing my wound and eating dinner, Coronado started barking furiously at something outside. We looked out the window but it was too dark to see anything. As a precaution, Grandma made sure the folding bus door was securely locked. Shortly afterward, our worst fears were realized. Something very large started smashing into the bus door causing Coronado to go into a frenzy trying to go after whatever was out there. This made the creature outside even more aggressive and it looked like the door wouldn't hold shut much longer from the intense pounding. With the exception of my brother, we were all screaming hysterically and I thought for sure we were going to be eaten alive by a wild animal. In order to better secure the door, we threw some objects at its base, wedging them between the bottom of the first step and the door. This seemed to help. The pounding gradually turned into an eerie scratching noise that sounding like fingernails on a chalk board. Then as quickly as it started the attacker was gone, and an uneasy silence filled the cabin of our bus with the exception of Coronado still barking intermittently, with the memory of all the action still fresh on his mind. We all couldn't believe what had just happened and I'll guarantee you that none of us hardly slept a wink the rest of the night.

When morning finally arrived, we inspected the outside of the door which had large scratch marks that reached over six feet tall. A bear is the only animal that could have reached that high and large tracks found in the soft mud around the bus confirmed this. The smell of our dinner being prepared probably brought the bear in for a closer look and when it heard Coronado barking, it became aggressive and tried to get at him. That experience has never left me, and to this day, I am cautious while in bear country.

✝ ✝ ✝

Grandpa took his goldmine very seriously and made frequent trips that required a lot of hard work in hopes of striking the mother lode. Off and on, he spent the rest of his life, even into his late 80's, searching and dreaming for that promised gold but never found it. Prospecting was just one of many things he enjoyed. His biggest passion was flying his airplane. I once asked Grandpa what he liked the most about living in an age of modern technology. He quickly replied, "The thermostat on the wall." I thought that was pretty funny. It makes sense when you realize that he grew up in a generation where they had to keep a wood or coal-fired stove burning to stay warm, even if it meant waking up in the middle of the night – that was one thing he would never miss. Instead of finding the mother lode, he left us with a wonderful family legacy that will be enjoyed by generations to come. Grandpa passed away at 90 years old and I look forward to being reunited with him in Heaven.

† † †

Regarding my dad, one could ask the question – would it have been better if Mom didn't marry him but instead married a Christian? The answer is probably yes, but the wonder of God is His ability to take our poor decisions and make them work out for the best. (Romans 8:28)

> *And we know that in all things God works for the good of those who love him, who have been called according to his purpose.*

Just because we choose a Christian doesn't mean things will work out, but it can definitely increase our chances for a successful relationship, and it allows us to be more obedient to God. Unfortunately, some of us think we know better so we spend a good portion of our time trying to change the other person. This is rarely accomplished and usually leads to years of frustration resulting in a failed relationship. Because He has given us a free will, not even God can force us to change, so why do we think we can do better? We would be much better off if we just learned to accept the other person for who they are instead of trying to change them into the person we want them to become. This is much easier said than done and I struggle with this on a daily basis.

Addictions

Growing up watching my dad struggle with his smoking and drinking addiction showed me first hand what these potentially devastating diseases can do to people as well as the damage it can cause to those living around them. My sister was heavily into gymnastics and unfortunately she had a coach that constantly told her she was fat and needed to lose weight. This couldn't have been further from the truth, but my sister was very impressionable in her young age, and took what her coach said to heart despite all of us telling her that it simply wasn't true. My sister developed a severe case of bulimia, an eating disorder that causes people to eat large quantities of food and then throw it up immediately afterwards. For a period of time, this dangerous, life-controlling illness completely consumed her.

By the grace of God, several days after being prayed over by an evangelical preacher, our Lord came to her in a still, small voice and told her that she was healed. My sister was very fortunate to have had an army of people praying for her which resulted in a powerful miracle from our Lord. This changed her life and allowed her to be a faithful witness to others with this problem. She even had the opportunity to share her testimony on the 700 Club.

Through research, we learned that young girls in particular have a much greater chance of becoming bulimic when their fathers are alcoholics. Alcoholic fathers tend to spend more time on their addiction than they do fostering a relationship with their daughters. Research has proven that the relationship between the father and daughter is essential for the well-being and confidence

41

of a young woman. These experiences taught me first hand that alcoholism not only affects the alcoholic, but all who are associated with them. By the grace of God, our family is now free from this curse and I pray for all those addicted that God will deliver them.

We would all do much better following God's commandments. These laws were not given to control or restrict us, but rather to protect and guide us through our journey in life. Many problems could be avoided if we would just be more patient and open to God's perfect plan for us. Following Christ Jesus should not be limited to a few things but should include every aspect of our lives including the relationships we enter into.

Our Bodies

What we put into our bodies such as food and drink should be carefully considered because our bodies are the temple of the Holy Spirit. We have a spiritual and physical responsibility to take good care of ourselves and should exercise self-control in the quantity and quality of the food and drink we consume on a daily basis. To disrespect our body is a sin against God who created us. On the other hand, becoming obsessed with our body's health and appearance can be just as damaging. As Christians, we need to find the balance that glorifies God by allowing us to be in good spiritual and physical condition. (Isaiah 55:2), (2 Corinthians 7:1)

> *Why spend money on what is not bread, and your labor on what does not satisfy? Listen, listen to me, and eat what is good, and your soul will delight in the richest of fare.*

> *Since we have these promises, dear friends, let us purify ourselves from everything that contaminates body and spirit, perfecting holiness out of reverence for God.*

The Apostle Paul emphasizes spiritual training as the most important attribute. (1 Timothy 4:8)

> *For physical training is of some value, but godliness has value for all things, holding promise for both the present life and the life to come.*

In light of the above, how can Christians justify becoming addicted to something that can cause harm to their bodies and souls? Smoking is one addiction that is extremely difficult to break. My dad was able to quit drinking, but never came close to stop smoking. In my opinion, it is a powerful addiction that needs prayer and fasting along with medical help to overcome. Dad's inability and/or desire to stop smoking tragically took his life with lung cancer at the early age of 52.

The way our body is perceived by others causes most of us great concern. Unfortunately, the media has bombarded us with their version of the perfect image. When we perceive ourselves as not meeting that image it can cause despair, even to the point of eating disorders and in extreme situations, it can lead to suicidal behaviors. How others perceive us is very important to us. We have become so obsessed with this that people in our country and abroad are spending billions of dollars on cosmetic surgery and other means to try and meet these expectations placed upon them. It is good to be well groomed and for us to maintain a healthy body, but have we gone too far with our vanity? 2 Timothy 3:2 in part tells us that in the last days,

> *. . . People will be lovers of themselves . . . .*

As Christians, where do we cross the line when placing too much emphasis on our bodies? Over doing it will only lead to despair because we will never be able to live up to our own or the world's expectations. We are seeking perfection but only God is perfect. It's ok to have features that don't meet the world's standards because we are all uniquely created in God's image and He loves us all the same no matter what we look like. (Samuel 16:6)

> But the LORD said to Samuel, "Do not consider his appearance or his height, for I have rejected him. The LORD does not look at the things man looks at. Man looks at the outward appearance, but the LORD looks at the heart."

It is true that those who are beautiful according to the world's standards may have an easier time being accepted by others. This acceptance is sometimes not out of respect for them, but rather, out of insecurity. People in general want to be associated with others who make themselves look good. This is unfortunate because looks are only one small part of a person's total makeup.

As a result, our obsession with outward appearances has become more important than how qualified a person is. This is especially true in politics. How many well qualified people never get a chance to share their talents because of this unjust discrimination? How many potentially great leaders have been shunned away because their outward appearance did not meet the status quo? It's unfortunate that so many positions of importance, especially those in the public spotlight have been reduced to a beauty contest. Only after meeting this requirement do some of us consider the merits of the person seeking the position. Society has become so accustomed to scrutinizing the outward appearance that the inward qualities, which are the most important, have taken a back seat.

As Christians, it's ok if we don't meet the worldly expectations placed upon us because it's not the world that we serve. God is our master and each one of us has been created in his image. He gives each one of us unique strengths to successfully carry out our lives. Some of us may not have outward beauty but have been blessed with other characteristics that are equally, if not more important.

Instead of driving ourselves crazy by focusing on what we don't have, we should put our efforts on our strengths. We cannot have it all because our world is not perfect – only in Heaven will we be completely satisfied. Seeking perfection will only lead to a miserable, frustrating life.

To avoid falling into this trap, we need to accept who we are, and be thankful to God for giving us life. Our Lord can smooth out the rough edges and shape us into the person he wants us to be. He will more than make up for any of our weaknesses. We cannot think for a moment that being more beautiful or more talented will make us any happier because our happiness does not rely on our circumstances. True happiness can only come from our relationship with God.

Our Minds

What we allow into our minds directly affects who we are and what we believe in. If we watch or read material that has information contrary to our faith, it becomes easier for us to become influenced by secular ideologies, many times without us even being aware of it. You've heard the expression, "You are what you eat." The same is true for what we allow into our minds.

Back when I was in college, I remember just how influential professors were to their students, especially to those in their first year of studies. Looking around the classroom, I could see all the mesmerized faces staring at the teacher, soaking up all the information like a sponge with their young impressionable minds. This would be a good thing if the information was consistent with God's Word, but unfortunately, some of the lessons being taught were aimed at convincing students that the existence of a supreme God was not necessary for the origination of our universe.

I attended a creative writing course where my professor introduced us to the concept of existentialism. I never knew the word even existed let alone what it meant. At first I was interested in learning more about it, but as my professor went further into his lecture on this subject I realized that existentialism wasn't for me. He explained it as a philosophical ideology where an individual believes there is no proof for a higher creator; therefore, humanity is here for no inherent purpose so we are free to choose whatever form of value/morality system we desire. To me, this was a very depressing outlook on life and I wondered how many students in my class were being influenced by this empty philosophy. Our professor disclosed to the class that he was completely sold on this form of atheism and that he had been religiously following it for some time. After finishing his lecture, he gave us a writing assignment on the topic.

I asked myself how I could write about something in a positive way that I completely disagreed with. I didn't want to upset the teacher but I didn't see any other way to go about it without compromising my faith. I ended up attacking existentialism on all fronts by quoting past and present scientists and philosophers who argued the need for a divine creator to explain life.

Albert Einstein

Albert Einstein, one of the most brilliant scientists of our age, was the focal point of my argument against existentialism. Even though he was thought to be a professed deist rather than a believer in a personal God, I used several of his well known quotes in my paper where he implied that he could not turn his back on the need for a supreme intelligence to explain the laws and order of the universe. In the following article from the Saturday Evening Post Magazine, Albert Einstein expresses his views on Christianity, intuition, and inspiration in an interview with George Sylvester Viereck:

> Einstein: "... I believe in intuitions and inspirations. I sometimes feel that I am right. I do not know that I am ...."

Viereck: "Then you trust more to your imagination than to your knowledge?"

Einstein: "I am enough of an artist to draw freely upon my imagination. Imagination is more important than knowledge. Knowledge is limited. Imagination encircles the world."

Viereck: "To what extent are you influenced by Christianity?"

Einstein: "As a child I received instruction in both the Bible and in the Talmud. I am a Jew but I am enthralled by the luminous figure of the Nazarene."
Viereck: "Have you read Emil Ludwig's book on Jesus?"

Einstein: "Emil Ludwig's Jesus," Einstein replied, "is shallow. Jesus is too colossal for the pen of phrasemongers, however artful. No man can dispose of Christianity with a bon mot."

Viereck: "You accept the historical existence of Jesus?"

Einstein: "Unquestionably. No one can read the gospels without feeling the actual presence of Jesus. His personality pulsates in every word. No myth is filled with such life."

Viereck: ". . . Ludwig Lewisohn, in one of his recent books, claims many of the sayings of Jesus paraphrase the sayings of other prophets."

Einstein: "No man," Einstein replied, "can deny the fact that Jesus existed, nor that his sayings are beautiful. Even if some of them have been said before, no one has expressed them as divinely as he."

Viereck: "Gilbert Chesterton told me that, according to a Catholic writer in a Dublin Review, your theory of relatively merely confirms the cosmology of Thomas Aquinas."

Einstein: "I have not," Einstein replied, "read all the works of Thomas Aquinas, but I am delighted if I have reached the same conclusions as the comprehensive mind of that great Catholic scholar . . . ."

Viereck: ". . . Your modesty," I remarked, "does you credit."

Einstein: "No," Einstein replied with a shrug of his shoulders. "I claim credit for nothing. Everything is determined, the beginning as well as the end, by forces over which we have no control. It is determined for the insect as well as for the star. Human beings, vegetables, or cosmic dust, we all dance to a mysterious tune, intoned in the distance by an invisible player." [3]

My professor ended up giving me a failing grade on my paper even though I thought it was well written. I had obviously hurt his feelings by not agreeing with his personal philosophy so he felt the need to punish me. After class, I went up to him and asked why he thought I had done so poorly on the assignment and he claimed it was due to poor grammar and content. While talking with him, I noticed he was extremely nervous which also made me uncomfortable in his presence. I asked if I could correct the

---

3   Viereck, George S. "An Interview by George Sylvester Viereck." *The Saturday Evening Post Magazine* 26 Oct. 1929: 117+. Print. "The Saturday Evening Post magazine, © 1929. Saturday Evening Post Society. Used with permission."

assignment to improve my grade and he rejected my offer. This was unfortunate because I really liked this professor – we had a lot in common as both of us really enjoyed the outdoors, particularly while observing and photographing wildlife. Through my required daily journal, I often shared stories with him of my experiences while out in the field, but it seemed a rift had developed between us too wide to cross again. Fortunately, after it was all said and done, I ended up getting an A in the course, but more importantly, we became friends and he taught me a lot about writing.

† † †

Throughout my college years, I had several courses, especially in the sciences, where the professor would lecture on controversial topics. As time went on, I developed the courage to challenge their views in front of the class. I had one teacher who got so used to me commenting that after he finished with a main point, he would ask me, with a grin on his face, if I had anything to add to his discussion. The class would just laugh because they knew that I would have a reply that probably wouldn't be what the professor wanted to hear. Once I commented, others in the class would also join in which resulted in some healthy debates.

The Theory of Evolution was one of the main subjects continually pounded into the heads of students. Out of all my professors, only one of them told us that God could have used evolution for the creation of life. The rest of them taught chance evolution as if it were fact even though it is just a theory. Even if some of them wanted to include God in their discussion, they feared the threat of being fired if they mentioned His name. If a student didn't already have a strong foundation in our Lord, they were easy prey for this Godless chance theory that was/is taught in most of our public schools, including the lecture halls of our colleges and universities.

This is a powerful force to overcome even if we are Christian. That is why I encourage all Christians to have the courage to stand up for our beliefs, even if it means respectfully challenging our professors and teachers no matter what grade we're in. It may be the only time some of these students ever hear the real truth. The sad thing is, Christians are not standing up enough while millions of students each year are being brainwashed by the secular world that God is not needed anymore.

Secular science thinks it has come up with a theory that excludes God from the equation by replacing Him with random chance events. If you really study what they are proclaiming here, it exposes how ridiculous it is to rely on something as chaotic as chance to prove how life originated. Ridiculous or not, Evolution has taken over as the predominant theory replacing God in the minds of secular thinkers.

Because it is being taught at such an early age, this Godless ideology is adversely affecting entire generations of people, including Christians. I feel it is partly responsible for the break down of marriages, families, and the overall break down of moral behavior in society. We cannot take our Lord out of the picture and expect life to go smoothly. After all, He is the only reason why we have life to begin with.

In order to live a successful Christian life, we have a moral responsibility to guard what we allow into our hearts and minds. Everything must be tested with God's Word. (Proverbs 4:23), (1Thessalonians 5: 21-22)

> Above all else, guard your heart, for it is the wellspring of life.

> Test everything. Hold on to the good. Avoid every kind of evil.

Chapter 3

Evolution

When I was in college, most of my science professors pushed the theory that all living organisms originated from primordial soup millions of years ago, and over time, mutated from the simplest building block of a cell into complex living organisms through a process called natural selection. In other words, the majority of them claimed that all life originated from random chance events thereby eliminating the need for God to explain our existence. Even though the truth of this theory may seem far fetched considering the overwhelming odds against it, Evolution has taken over as the predominant scientific explanation for life, and unfortunately, has little or no academic competition within the public school system. Whether we agree or disagree with this theory does not change the fact that it will continue to be pounded into our children's and young adults' minds throughout their educational careers.

Suddenly, in our generation, the world is telling us that we do not need God for our existence. For some this may not be a big deal, but for others it can plant the seed of doubt that can ultimately destroy their faith. In reality, Evolution has missing links and gaps the size of outer space.

One of my favorite books exposing the holes in Evolution is *"Evolution from Space."* It was written in the 1970's by co-authors Sir Frederick Hoyle and Chandra Wickramasinghe. Sir Hoyle is a world-renowned British mathematician and astronomer, who calculated the mathematical probability of the spontaneous generation of simple enzymes from a primordial soup. His results concluded that the probability of this occurring to approximately 2000 enzymes in a chance trial is one part in 1040,000 which according to Sir Hoyle is, ". . . An outrageously small probability that could not be faced even if the whole universe consisted of organic soup."[4] Prior to conducting this analysis, both Sir Hoyle and Wickramasinghe believed in the spontaneous generation of life, but due to their conclusive results, they were compelled to change their minds. Instead, they felt it more logical that precise instruction through intelligent design was necessary for life to have assembled itself.[5]

Sir Hoyle's calculations only shed light on the simplest enzymes in the cell. He did not calculate the odds against highly complex structures such as DNA and RNA forming through spontaneous generation. The odds against their natural formation are even more mind boggling, and if we consider the entire human body, it becomes ridiculous. Why then does mainstream science persist when it is considered by respected scientists to be nearly impossible with overwhelming odds against it? It took a miracle for life to exist and few evolutionists would argue that point but they do not agree that intelligent design was the source of that miracle. Instead, they have credited it to blind chance.

Scientists have a difficult time accepting information that cannot be tested within the laws of nature; therefore, science has limited itself to the known and has left the unknown to philosophers, theologians, and others to interpret. The idea that God created

---

4   Hoyle, Sir Fred, and Chandra N. Wickremasinghe. *Evolution From Space.* New York, New York : Simon and Schuster , 1981. *24.* Print.

5   Hoyle, Sir Fred, and Chandra N. Wickremasinghe. *Evolution From Space.* New York, New York : Simon and Schuster , 1981. *30,31,150.* Print.

everything is presently incalculable through modern science; they can't put an equation to it and therefore, have rendered it as non-science. According to them, faith has no place in science, only equations and models that can lead to predictable outcomes and conclusions. The problem with Evolution is the enormous gaps not accounted for between species. Millions of years of necessary information are missing, and to help fill in these gaps, scientists rely on educated guesses. In reality, they are also reliant on faith, the very thing they claim to be against.

Perfectly Balanced Laws of Nature

In college, I had the opportunity to major in the environmental sciences and was overwhelmed at the complexity of even the simplest living cell and how much structure and order was/is integrated into their design. Not only did I find order in all living things, but in the nonliving environment as well. The Earth, planets, and galaxy in which we live are in near perfect balance. It is amazing to think that we can be sitting still in a lawn chair enjoying a warm sunny day sipping ice tea when in reality, we are being hurled around space at incredible speeds. It is also important to note that if any one of these speeds were to change, life on Earth would not be possible.

Our Earth is rotating around 1000 miles per hour and is orbiting around the sun approximately 67,000 miles per hour.[6] If the Earth's rotation was any faster or slower, the Coriolis Force (effects the direction of the Earth's air currents caused by the rotation of the Earth)[7] would be altered, which could drastically change the world's weather patterns in a way that could be unfavorable to life. If the Earth's rotation was slower, it is obvious that the length of

6   Butterworth, Paul , and David Palmer. "Ask an Astrophysicist." NASA's Imagine the Universe NASA, 7 Apr. 2007. Web. 03 Oct. 2007
    <http://imagine.gsfc.nasa.gov/docs/ask_astro/answers/970401c.html>.
7   "Wind." National Weather Service Forecast OfficeCorpus Christi, TX noaa, NA. Web. 31 Oct. 2009
    <http://www.srh.noaa.gov/crp/weather/education/wind.html>.

night and day would be longer, subjecting the Earth to extreme hot and cold spots which would be detrimental to living things. If the Earth's orbit around the Sun was any closer or farther from its existing position, it would be logical to predict that our planet would lose its temperate climate and would become too hot or cold like Venus and Mars, respectively.

Our Milky Way Galaxy is traveling through space at approximately 1.4 million miles per hour.[8] Now that is really fast! Our Earth is tilted on its axis approximately 23.5 degrees which is due primarily to the gravitational pull of our Moon. A few degrees more tilt, our climate fluctuations would be too severe, any less, our four seasons would be eliminated.[9] The Moon is also the perfect size and distance in relation to the Earth. Due to its gravitational pull on the Earth, if the Moon were any closer, large tidal changes would flood the Earth's coasts.3[10] Common sense tells us that if the Moon was any further away, shorelines would become stagnant, causing many animal species to become extinct. The size of the Earth, Moon, Sun, other planets, and even our galaxy had to be just right in order for the Earth to have life. I've only listed a few out of many problems that would result from even the slightest change to the physical world around us.

Could all of this just be a coincidence or does creation cry out for a creator? We need to think long and hard about what evolutionists are proclaiming. The list of things that had to happen before life could exist goes on and on.

---

8   Graduate Department, University of Hawaii. "X-rays Reveal What Makes the Milky Way Move." University of Hawaii, Institute for Astronomy University of Hawaii, 11 Jan. 2006. Web. 22 Aug. 2007
     <http://www.ifa.hawaii.edu/info/press-releases/kocevski-1-06/>.
9   "What causes the earth to experience different seasons?." National Oceanic and Atmospheric Administration National Data Buoy Center NOAA, 18 June 2002. Web. 15 Sep. 2007
     <http://www.ndbc.noaa.gov/educate/seasons.shtml>
10   Odenwald , Sten. "Earth- Rotation, question 18." Ask The Space Scientist NASA, NA. Web. 31 Oct. 2009
     <http://image.gsfc.nasa.gov/poetry/ask/askmag.html>.

E = MC²

$E = MC^2$ is probably one of the best known physics equations in the world. Albert Einstein came up with this brilliant equation derived from his Theory of Relativity. It basically states that matter and energy are really just different forms of the same thing; therefore, they can be turned into one another.[11] It also states that it only takes a small amount of matter to be transformed in order to release a tremendous amount of energy – thus the advent of the atomic bomb.[12]

$E = MC^2$ defined:

> (E)nergy = (M)ass times the speed of light squared (C squared) in a vacuum.
>
> The speed of light is approximately 300,000,000 (m)eters/(s)econd or 186,000 miles/second).[13]

The above equation seems simple enough but the things that can be discovered from this are endless. It has revolutionized the way science thinks about the universe.

Gravity

Sir Isaac Newton discovered the force of gravity on all objects. From his discovery, science understands how to calculate its effects but they really do not understand what it is.4[14] We are

---

11 Butterworth, Paul , and David Palmer. "Ask an Astrophysicist." NASA's Imagine the Universe NASA, 26 Mar. 1997. Web. 19 Sep. 2008 <http://imagine.gsfc.nasa.gov/docs/ask_astro/answers/970326a4.html>.

12 Waldrop, Mitchell M. "World Year of Physics 2005 - Circle: E=mc2." National Science Foundation NSA, 2005. Web. 27 Sept. 2008 <http://www.nsf.gov/news/special_reports/wyop/textonly.jsp>.

13 Rosenvinge, Dr. Tycho v. "Speed of Light." Cosmicopia - an abundance of cosmic rays NASA, 29 Dec. 2006. Web. 22 Sep. 2008 <http://helios.gsfc.nasa.gov/gloss_st.html>.

14 Dejoie , Joyce , and Elizabeth Truelove. "What is Gravity?." StarChild Question of the Month for February 2001 NASA, Feb. 2001. Web. 22 Sep. 2008 <http://starchild.gsfc.nasa.gov/docs/StarChild/questions/question30.html>.

fortunate that the force of gravity is constant in our universe. More powerful, it would rip us apart, any less, we wouldn't have an atmosphere blanketing our planet. God made His laws of nature reliable and understandable so human kind would have the perfect conditions to live on Earth, and at the same time, be able to study his creation. A universe that resulted from chance evolution could not have accounted for the precision and reliability of the laws of nature; only a supreme intelligent designer could. Little by little God reveals his wonder at the proper time.

Water, Ice, and Snow

Another amazing and rare occurrence in the physical world is the formation of ice. Ice defies the natural laws of solids. Almost all other elements increase in density (heavier) when they solidify (become a solid), but water on the other hand becomes less dense (lighter) when it becomes a solid.[15] This is important because if ice was heavier than liquid water, it would sink to the bottom of lakes and rivers forming layer upon layer, eventually causing the entire body of water to freeze solid. The end result would be catastrophic to all aquatic life. Thankfully, God thought of everything. He made an exception to His natural law by allowing ice to float on top of the water, thereby insulating the underlying area which provides an environment suitable for life, even in the harshest conditions.

What about snow? After picking my son up from high school he made a random comment that really got me thinking about chance evolution. It was the beginning of January and we recently had a series of storms that dumped nearly two feet of snow in our area. We finally had a break in the weather and the snow was starting to melt on the side of the road. My son noticed this and he said, "Good thing snow is white so it doesn't melt too fast. The snow that's stained black from the road is melting a lot quicker than

15 Rennie, Gabriele. "Revealing the Mysteries of Water - A Common Substance with Unusual Properties." University of California, Science and Technology US Department of Energy, 7 Oct. 2005. Web. 10 Nov. 2008 <https://www.llnl.gov/str/October05/Mundy.html>.

the clean white snow." His comment may sound simplistic, but if snow were any darker in color, the polar ice caps would not exist today because the darker color would absorb more of the Sun's energy resulting in rapid melting. We would also prematurely lose sustained snow pack in the high country which would lead to rapid runoff, causing severe flooding and later followed by drought conditions.[16] White just happens to be the perfect color to reflect the Sun's energy. This preserves the snow and ice longer allowing for a gradual, sustained runoff well into the summer season. It also helps keep entire snow-covered regions cooler by reflecting the Sun's energy back out to space. Entire climates would be detrimentally impacted if this were not the case.

Again, are we just lucky that snow is the perfect color or is there an intelligent designer that is behind all the above so-called coincidences? If only a few things in our universe required chance, I might be more willing to give it some consideration, but when everything around us, including our bodies are in near perfect order, chance evolution simply cannot be the explanation. Rather, in my opinion, it is obvious to the most impartial observer that intelligent design is likely responsible for our ordered existence.

My Theory of Proportionality in All Things

It took intelligent design for manmade objects to be constructed in proper proportions to the size of humans. An average door is built at a certain height to prevent most of us from hitting our heads while entering a building. A baseball is designed to allow a pitcher to get a good grip on the ball which is necessary to accurately throw the ball in the strike zone. Automobiles, bicycles, clothing, fixtures, electronics, and endless other items have also been specifically customized to meet our needs.

---

16 DOE/Pacific Northwest National Laboratory. "Dirty Snow Causes Early Runoff In Cascades, Rockies." ScienceDaily 13 January 2009. 06 mar. 2009 <http://www.sciencedaily.com/releases/2009/01/090112093336.htm>.

The same characteristics can be observed in our natural environment including humans, plants, animals, the Earth, and other celestial bodies throughout our universe. I give several examples in this chapter that illustrate how perfectly proportionate these things are in comparison to each other, and if studied closely, this fact demands intelligent design for a rational explanation. Not only do we have proper proportions, but an element of beauty and convenience has been factored in allowing humans to further appreciate life.

What if the sky was always a dull grey color or if flowers consisted of only one generic shade? We could probably still survive in such a bland environment but our quality of life would not be the same. Fortunately for us, our world is full of vibrant colors that are pleasing to the eye. We are also fortunate that the Earth is located in an area of our spiral galaxy that is ideal for observing celestial bodies close to home and deep into outer space.[17] Our location also happens to be protected from the dangers of space. Not only are we able to safely survive in our given location and environment, we also have the opportunity to observe and study our natural surroundings. It appears that someone intended for us to enjoy our surroundings and to understand how the universe was created.[18]

In my opinion, the human body is also in perfect proportion to our natural surroundings. It appears that humans were the model and everything else was designed around it. The size and skeletal structure of a horse is one of the best arguments for this case. Was it just an accident that a mature horse is just the right size for most people to mount and ride for short or long distances? Was it also luck that a horse's backbone is slightly swayed in a reversed

---

17 Gonzalez , Guillermo , and Jay Richards. "Introduction to the Privileged Planet." The Privileged Planet Regnery Publishing, 15 June 2005. Web. 22 Oct. 2007 <http://www.discovery.org/a/2677>.

18 Richards , Jay , and Guillermo Gonzalez. "The American Spectator - Are We Alone?". The Privileged Planet N.p., 1 May 2004. Web. 22 Oct. 2007 <http://www.discovery.org/a/2143>.

arch position, allowing a rider to comfortably fit on its back, even without a saddle?

Compared to the Earth, we are microscopic in size, but fortunately for us, everything else around us including the mountains, trees, grasses, flowers, rivers, lakes, animals, and even the celestial bodies were made in perfect proportion to our size. We are not too big to miss out on the details of a lady bug crawling on a blade of grass, and we are not too small to be able to witness a beautiful sunset on the distant horizon, or to climb a rugged mountain peak above timberline. In other words, God has made humans and the natural world around us the best possible size for us to actually participate in His creation. This allows us to observe a wide variety of characteristics, from a grain of sand, to distant galaxies.

Ants couldn't do this even if they were intelligent enough because they are limited by their physiological features. Eagles have excellent vision but probably pay little attention to the stars above unless they are using them for navigational purposes. It's all about survival for animal species but humans stand unique because we have the ability to go beyond our temporal needs and have a strong desire to discover and learn about the world around us.

Just imagine if our world was out of proportion. What if ocean waves were consistently 100 feet tall? It would be difficult to enjoy a day at the beach without risking your life. As mentioned earlier, this is exactly what would happen if the Moon was larger or closer to the Earth. What if the smallest dogs were as large as grizzly bears or if deer were carnivorous and stood 30 feet tall, or if a common squirrel was the size of a mountain lion, or worse yet, mosquitoes were as big as eagles? It could make a walk in the woods a terrifying experience. Fortunately for us, God created everything in proper proportions allowing us to enjoy His creation instead of fearing it. We have only scratched the surface in our understanding of our world and the possibilities of new discoveries are endless.

It is my theory that all living and non-living things in the universe are in perfect proportion to one another. This would include everything from simple bacteria to distant galaxies. If true, the odds that chance could have been responsible for this outcome would be nearly impossible. Rather, it is more logical to hold intelligent design responsible due to the overwhelming complexity involved if everything in the universe is similar through proportionality.

Beneficial Application Using Similar Triangles

Using basic laws of geometry, we know that **corresponding sides of similar triangles are proportional if their corresponding angles are congruent.**[19]

Figure 1

Austrian Pine
Tree Height

Human Height

A

X

B   53'   C

D

6'

E   8'   F

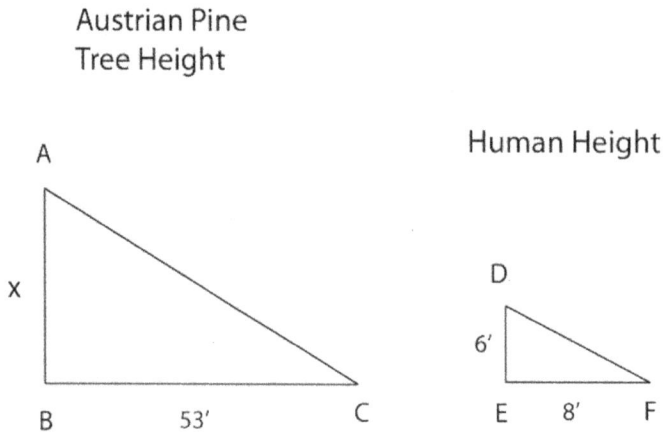

$\triangle ABC \sim \triangle DEF \rightarrow AB/DE = BC/EF = AC/DF$

19 Odenwald , Dr. Sten. "Angular Size and Similar Triangles." Space Math @ NASA NASA, ?. Web. 17 Dec. 2007
<http://spacemath.gsfc.nasa.gov/weekly/6Page28.pdf>.

Drawing from this information and assuming proportionality between all things, humans are similar to all species and natural objects in relation to their proportional size. Therefore, using the above geometric law, we can use the height or depth of a human or any other object as a means in determining the unknown measurement of another species or natural object by creating a situation where their corresponding angles are congruent.

One beneficial application would be to use this information to find the unknown height of an Austrian Pine tree. It would be difficult to measure the height of a tree with a tape measure making it more practical to use your body as a scale model to achieve the desired result. This could be accomplished by using the well known shadow method.

The first step would be to measure the length of the base created by a shadow cast on the ground from both the human body and the pine tree. The degree of the angle formed at the top of each object would be the same as long as the objects were measured at the same time and location. This satisfies the requirement that the opposing angles must be congruent (equivalent). Therefore, we can modify the above geometric law as follows: **Corresponding heights or depths of similar species and natural objects are proportional if their corresponding angles are congruent.**

Solving the Problem

After measuring the length of the shadow cast along ground from the Austrian Pine tree, we come up with 53'. Using a human body height of 6', it casts a shadow approximately 8' along the ground. Using **Figure 1 above,** we group together the appropriate combination of lettered coordinates to solve the equation.

> The Austrian Pine tree height is **AB**, and the length of the shadow cast on the ground by the pine tree is **BC**.

The height of the human body is **DE**, and length of the shadow cast along the ground by the body is **EF**.

We want to find the height of the pine tree which is **AB**.

Using a portion of the equation in **Figure 1 above**, we plug the known measurements into the following equation and solve using basic algebra:

AB/DE = BC/EF[20]

AB/6' = 53'/8' =
AB = 53'/8' * 6' =
AB = 6.625' * 6' =
AB = 39.75'

Or more simply put:

tree height(x)/shadow length = human height/ shadow length

Substituting in the known values and solving for x we have:

x/53' = 6'/8'=
x = 6'/8'* 53' =
x = .75' * 53' =
x = 39.75'

Therefore, the Austrian Pine Tree is approximately 39.75' tall in both examples.

This technique can be used for determining the height or depth of any object as long as there is enough information available

---

20 Cohen , Kathleen. "How Tall is That?." NASA Ames Research Center NASA, 28 Sep. 2000. Web. 29 Oct. 2007 <http://geo.arc.nasa.gov/sge/ jskiles/top- down/how_tall_that_is/how_tall_is_that.html>.

to apply basic algebra and trigonometry necessary to solve the equation. The above work does not necessarily prove that all things are proportionate, but rather, demonstrates how dependable the natural laws in the universe are for predicting outcomes.

This also shows us a beneficial application when using proportionality. In my opinion, the precise order in our universe could not have come from random chance. Rather, it is far more likely that intelligence is behind this wonderful mystery. If I were better at math, I feel confident I could prove through a statistical equation that the precise proportionality existing between all species and the natural universe would be impossible if left to chance. Claiming that life is just an accident defies common sense and is an insult to humanity and to our Creator.

How Did it Happen?

Some ask if God could have used the process of evolution for His creation. In theory, this scenario is possible but unfortunately, secular science will not recognize the possibility of an intelligent designer. Instead, they only focus on random chance for answers. Therefore, Evolution is rarely taught with an intelligent designer in mind. In fact, it has come to the point where chance evolution has no competition in our schools. This is the only theory being taught and if you try and mention an intelligent designer as an explanation, you might risk being fired if you are a teacher or possibly failing the class if you are a student. It's as if they are terrified of the truth and will do anything to keep God out of the classroom long enough to come up with something that will convince everyone they're right. I would be able to tolerate this if they would at least acknowledge the need for intelligent design to be added to the equation. They are light years from convincing me that chance evolution is fact. Don't get me wrong, we need to embrace solid scientific principles that have been proven to be fact. However, the Theory of Evolution is not a proven fact and is open for debate. It needs to be thoroughly tested and compared to other competing models such as Intelligent Design.

I believe chance evolutionists would have a better argument if they claimed that aliens from another world created the Earth and its inhabitants. At least in that scenario, intelligent design is in play. In some cases, modern science has gone so far as to think the survival of humanity completely relies on their ability to figure out a way to save us. I don't think they truly understand what they are getting themselves into. That's one reason they're so terrified of an asteroid or super nova that could destroy the Earth at any instant, because they believe we're on our own, and it is up to science to save the world from any impending doom. What a tremendous burden to place on humanity.

Christians on the other hand believe that God is in control of every little detail in the universe and could easily divert an asteroid on a collision course with the Earth if He chooses. Or, God can give us the necessary technology at the right moment in history allowing us to divert an asteroid. Worse yet, God could allow an asteroid to hit the Earth as a form of judgment. I don't worry about natural disasters near as much as those caused by man. Nuclear war is first on my list. It is unimaginable that human kind has developed a technology that can destroy the Earth many times over. It gets even worse when we realize the type of people and nations who have access to weapons of mass destruction. If it weren't for God intervening on our behalf, I feel certain we would have already destroyed ourselves with these weapons. Fortunately, God is in control and is looking out for us.

Many scientists believe that an asteroid hit the Earth in prehistoric times that possibly killed off most of the dinosaurs. If this theory is true, maybe God allowed it to happen to make way for humans? The proposed impact didn't wipe out all the animals living during that time such as alligators, sharks, turtles, frogs, snakes, and mosquitoes which are still with us today. It was mainly the larger animals that became extinct. For obvious reasons, humans would have had a hard time co-existing with larger dinosaurs if we lived together during the same time period.

Micro Verses Macro Evolution

If animals were suppose to have evolved from one species to another (macroevolution)[21] then why are certain species mentioned above such as alligators, still essentially the same animal after millions of years of existence?[22]

If macroevolution were true, why are alligators still alligators? Of course minor adaptations have taken place (microevolution)[23] but these micro-changes didn't turn an alligator into a dog. Macroevolution is only a theory whereas microevolution is a fact. The genetics of all living creatures have been preprogrammed (requires intelligent design), which enables species to evolve certain micro-characteristics essential for them to adapt to their changing environments, helping to ensure their long-term survival. We can clearly see examples of this through our long time traditions in breeding dogs. In the medical field, we can observe certain strains of bacteria becoming resistant to specific antibiotics meant to kill them. Chance evolutionists tell us this ability comes from a process called natural selection. Merriam-Webster's Online Dictionary defines natural selection as, "A natural process that results in the survival and reproductive success of individuals or groups best

21 "macroevolution" Merriam-Webster Online Dictionary. 2009. Merriam-Webster Online. 20 January 2009 http://www.merriam-webster.com/dictionary/macroevolution .By permission. From the Merriam-Webster Online Dictionary © 2009 by Merriam-Webster, Incorporated. <www.merriam-web.com>.

22 "Dinosaurs, Ancient Fossils, New Discoveries, Extinction." American Museum of Natural History N.p., 14 May 2005. Web. 23 Nov. 2007 <http://www.amnh.org/exhibitions/dinosaurs/extinction/dinosaurs.php>.

23 "microevolution," Merriam-Webster Online Dictionary. 2009. Merriam-Webster Online. 20 January 2009 <http://www.merriam- webster.com/dictionary/microevolution>. By permission. From the Merriam-Webster Online Dictionary © 2009 by Merriam-Webster, Incorporated. <www.merriam-web.com>.

adjusted to their environment and that leads to the perpetuation of genetic qualities best suited to that particular environment."[24]

I do not disagree with the basic fundamentals of natural selection. However, common sense tells us that species do not have any ability to make these changes on their own, and in my opinion, they certainly do not rely on chance mutations to perfect certain traits necessary for their survival. Simple logic would tell us that if it were left to chance, all species would quickly become extinct.

Even if a chance mutation occurred that benefited a particular species in one situation, another random event detrimental to that species would quickly follow, leading to its extinction. This is due to simple statistics. The odds of something becoming beneficial from chance mutations are remote while the odds of something harmful occurring are almost guaranteed. Rather, as stated above, it is more logical to think that these changes were preprogrammed by a designer who is responsible for their ability to adapt to a changing world.

We all know first hand what happens in our own lives when things are left to chance. Things literally fall apart around us, including our bodies, if we do not continually maintain them. Through practical experience, to think otherwise defies all reason. I used the above examples because it shows purpose and the necessity for a designer.

The next time we look up into the heavens, we should thank our mighty Creator for giving us such perfect order in our universe. If God pulled His hand from the wheel for just an instant, all life as we know it would be instantly destroyed. The same would be true on a much lesser scale if the wings on a jet blew off while traveling at 30,000 feet in the air.

---

24 "natural selection" Merriam-Webster Online Dictionary. 2009. Merriam-Webster Online. 20 January 2009 <http://www.merriam- webster.com/dictionary/natural%20selection>. By permission. From the Merriam-Webster Online Dictionary © 2009 by Merriam-Webster, Incorporated. <www.merriam- web.com>.

† † †

The more I studied in college, the more I realized the complexity of creation and how it would have been impossible for all of this to have been an accident. The evidence of a designer is written everywhere. For me, it would take a lot more faith to believe life happened by chance than it would to believe that an all powerful loving God created us and everything else in existence.

I felt it important to include a discussion on the Theory of Evolution because I feel that it is absolutely essential that Christians believe God is necessary for all life and everything that sustains it. Chance evolution plants the false seed of doubt that maybe God wasn't necessary for life. Doubt and unbelief separate us from Him. There is no excuse to not believe in God's creation because He made it so clear through its perfect order and design that only He could have accomplished such a spectacular feat. If we believe that God is in control of everything, we do not have to worry about asteroids or evil world leaders destroying the Earth. Rather, we can have peace knowing that He has everything under control and the only thing we need to do is trust in Him by being obedient to His powerful Word. Scripture confirms this in the following verse. (Romans 1:20)

> For since the creation of the world God's invisible qualities—his eternal power and divine nature—have been clearly seen, being understood from what has been made, so that men are without excuse.

Potential Consequences of Chance Evolution

If we follow the principles of chance evolution, it is only natural that human kind will do whatever it feels necessary to ensure its own survival, even if it is contrary to God's will. Some scientists have already begun to eliminate weak genetic characteristics in the gene pool and replace them with stronger, more viable alternatives. This is natural selection at its finest. Never before has any species been able to directly manipulate its own gene pool. Since the majority of secular academic institutions assume that life was just an accident, survival of the fittest is the bottom line. This helps to justify abortion, euthanasia, and unethical gene therapies used to create designer populations that are genetically superior. Adolph Hitler and other evil dictators used the same principles found in chance evolution to justify their atrocities against humanity. Now we are using the same rationalizations by aborting millions of unborn babies.

We are setting ourselves up for a disaster by playing God and the consequences could be catastrophic. We have no idea what we are getting ourselves into. Like the old saying goes, "We know just enough to get ourselves into trouble." It is like letting a baby drive a car by itself. The baby might be able to grab hold of the steering wheel but that is only one small step necessary to properly control the vehicle. With no perception to its surroundings, the baby would quickly run the car off the road. In certain cases, scientists are also only grabbing the steering wheel with no idea what implications might result from their actions.

If you look at this from the perspective of an evolutionist, we are only an accident with no real purpose or meaning with the exception of our own survival. In this perspective, you can see why they believe in what they are doing. It is only human instinct at work here. On the other hand, if there is a God, and as Christians we believe that there is, we have no excuse to follow the present culture of death. Instead, people from all walks of faith, including government leaders and scientists, have an obligation to help as many people as possible to see the real truth. We cannot continue to play a passive role. Instead, we need to get out and make a positive difference – the survival of those without a voice depends on it.

Intelligent Design Gaining Ground

There has recently been a movement amongst some scientists to consider Intelligent Design as a legitimate answer for the origin of life and our universe. New theories on Intelligent Design have been proposed using solid scientific models that make future predictions based on this information. I feel Intelligent Design will give Evolution a run for its money by providing much needed scientific truth and competition. It is my hope and prayer that Intelligent Design will eventually be taught in our schools, side by side with Evolution.

† † †

For more on how science affirms the Bible, you can check out *Reasons to Believe* on the Web at http://www.reasons.org. For an excellent non-biased book and film on our universe, I would highly recommend "*The Privileged Planet*" by Guillermo Gonzalez and Jay W. Richards. They present creation's need for a designer on a factual basis and in a way that is entertaining for all ages. Because of its scientific nature, it may be acceptable to be shown in public schools. For more information, check out their website at http://www.privilegedplanet.com/.

Challenging Evolution With Common Sense

Common sense is the best indicator of truth. A good example of this took place at my son's seventh-grade speech class. For one of his assignments, he brought in several pictures of various natural and manmade items. The first one was a picture of a natural sandstone arch in the desert. He then asked the class if the arch was created by intelligent design or by natural causes. Of course the class chose natural causes. The second picture was that of an arched bridge going over a large river. The class was asked the same question and the response was intelligent design. Next, a picture of some Indian writings etched into a cliff was displayed, and again the answer was intelligent design. Next a picture of the Empire State Building was displayed and the class unanimously answered intelligent design. This went on until finally a picture of the human body was shown.

At first, the class shouted out intelligent design but then quickly became divided in their answers. They had been told throughout their education that humans came from natural causes and trying to convince them otherwise was not an easy task. Someone else asked, "What are you trying to get at here?" My son then explained to them that he showed the pictures to illustrate how obvious it was to determine whether something was made by intelligent design or by natural causes. He went on further to illustrate how chance evolution is contrary to common sense. The class had a lengthy discussion on his topic and I'm sure it made some of them think in a different light. I learned a lot from his simple but powerful speech. Supernatural common sense is the answer to most of our questions in life.

Another example took place while my employee and I were digging a hole in the ground in preparation for a concrete pier. While digging, we came across an old metal screw that was heavily distorted with rust. I reached down and picked it up and carefully cleaned off the soil clinging to its perimeter. I thought of my son's speech and asked my employee if this object was created by intelligent design or was a result of chance? He quickly replied, "Intelligent design."

I asked him how he knew this and he said it was obvious because you could see the intricate spiral characteristics of a screw and went on to say that things that complex and ordered could not happen by chance. I smiled and asked him how he could believe we came from chance evolution if he thought something as simple as a screw could not have happened by chance. Earlier that day we had a serious debate over Evolution and he knew that I had just pinned him up against a wall – both of us just laughed and continued digging the hole.

Can you imagine the disappointment evolutionists experienced when the first probes landed on Mars and live images were sent back to Earth showing a landscape that past generations could only dream about; beautiful yes, but no apparent life forms were visible. Granted, scientists have barely scratched the surface and the possibility of life cannot yet be ruled out; however, it would be reasonable for an Intelligent Design theorist to make a future prediction that no life will be found on Mars unless that life form has served or serves a necessary purpose for the success of the planet. Our creator is a God of purpose and design and does not waste time on things with no meaning or function. Because of this, I personally do not believe that scientists will find even the simplest life form on Mars unless that life form came from Earth from a possible comet or asteroid collision or is essential for the proper function of the planet.

In the mean time, students are presently being taught that Evolution is not just a theory but is fact. This false concept couldn't be further from the truth and is contrary to good scientific principles. It is a fact that the Earth is somewhat round and has a gravitational force because it has been proven beyond a doubt and cannot be rationally contested. The Theory of Evolution is far from fact and may never be proven because the Earth, through its many cycles, is very efficient at removing evidence. Even if chance evolution was true (I personally do not believe it is), scientists will probably never be able to find enough missing evidence essential to their case because most of it has already been destroyed.

I do not have a problem with Evolution being taught as a theory and actually encourage it; however, the problem exists when other legitimate theories are discarded and Evolution remains in the driver's seat as the exclusive dominate theory with little or no competition. This type of behavior results in bad science and puts severe restraints on the truth. We need a choice here, not a monopoly.

It's no wonder some of our kids feel lost today; they are being exclusively taught that they are just an accident with no real meaning or purpose and are equivalent at best to any other animal species. What could be more degrading to children than that? How can we help offset these false truths that our children and young adults are exposed to on a daily basis? The answer is clear – we need to become more involved in their lives and explain to them that God exists, not only through our words but more importantly, through our actions. We also need to let them know that it is ok to challenge their teachers and others on this subject instead of just believing everything they are told. There is no guarantee that our kids will listen to us but if we don't do it, who will? We have a moral and spiritual obligation to make every effort to teach our children the truth. (Psalm 78:5-7)

> *He decreed statutes for Jacob and established the law in Israel, which he commanded our forefathers to teach their children,*
>
> *so the next generation would know them, even the children yet to be born, and they in turn would tell their children.*
>
> *Then they would put their trust in God and would not forget his deeds but would keep his commands.*

Chapter 4

Debt and Materialism

The following is a song (lyric) that my family and I wrote while traveling home from a vacation:

"It's Hard"

As I pulled out of the driveway I looked at all my stuff,
Sometimes I wonder will I ever have enough?
It's been six years and I have hardly been home,
I have a son and he's nearly half grown.

By the time I get back they're already asleep,
I'm totally exhausted, I'm beat!
I looked on the fridge and saw a little note,
Jimmy won his ball game; I had to clear my throat. Used to be so easy for my wife and me,
I'd take time out for the family.

It's hard, life's so hard!
Mortgage bills and credit cards, grocery bills, and expensive cars,
It's hard, life's so hard!

Can't take it any longer, can't keep living this way,
I got down on my knees and started to pray,

Kneeling on the floor I heard a sweet voice,
Was it an angel or another divine voice?
As I opened my eyes, my son was standing at the door.
He said "Daddy, what are you doing on the floor?" I said,"Son,
I think I've seen the light!"
I opened up my arms and hugged him real tight,

Thank God for showing me that a simple life with family,
Has brought me back to reality.
It's hard, life's so hard!

I've got a new outlook, I'm going to change some things,
With importance on family not material things.
I know it won't be easy, it'll still be hard,

But now I have purpose, thanks to our Lord.
I feel so excited! I feel so free!
A simple life with family.

It's hard, life's so hard!
Mortgage bills and credit cards,
Grocery bills and expensive cars,
It's hard, life's so hard!

A simple life with family,
Has brought me back to reality,
It's hard, life's so hard!

A simple life with family,
Has brought me back to reality,
It's hard, life's sooo harrrd!

A Cheerful Giver

This topic has such a powerful impact on Christians that I have dedicated a chapter to its discussion. First and foremost, we have to realize to whom our money belongs. (Psalm 24:1)

> *The earth is the LORD's, and everything in it, the world, and all who live in it . . . .*

Everything belongs to God including our money. We are blessed to have such a wonderful Creator who is generous and eager to share everything he has with us. However, we have to be careful to not take advantage of his kindness. Instead, we have to invest wisely and share what we have been given. (2 Corinthians 9:7)

> *Each man should give what he has decided in his heart to give, not reluctantly or under compulsion, for God loves a cheerful giver.*

Giving can be expressed through our prayers, time, talent, and treasure, but on some occasions it is better to be more specific in our giving. (James 2:15-16)

> *Suppose a brother or sister is without clothes and daily food. If one of you says to him, "Go, I wish you well; keep warm and well fed," but does nothing about his physical needs, what good is it?*

Update – August 2009

Recently, my wife and I had the opportunity to attend a benefit concert for LifeGuard. Funds were being raised to help them pay off the debt on their portable ultrasound machine. The ultrasound is used to show pregnant women who are contemplating an abortion their unborn baby as a living vibrant human being within them. According to the director of LifeGuard, almost 90% of the women contemplating an abortion who see the ultrasound of their unborn baby decide against it. This is an incredible success rate. Too much emphasis cannot be placed on the need to make sure portable ultrasound machines are placed in the hands of every pro- life clinic in our country and abroad.

Little did we know that one of the producers of the movie *Bella* would be in attendance helping out with the fundraiser. He surprised the audience by auctioning off the opportunity for a family to be able to be in one of their upcoming movies. All the proceeds would be going towards LifeGuard to help pay off their portable ultrasound machine. The producer also told the audience that to date, *Bella* has already saved at least 100 babies (that they know of) from being aborted. This is an impressive number and is a testimony to the life-saving impact this movie has had on women and men facing unwanted pregnancies.

The bid price for the opportunity to be in one of their new films ended up being fairly high. My wife looked over at me and said, "This is a once-in-a-lifetime opportunity and more importantly, it's going for a good cause." I had already planned on helping out but not quite at that level. Then I remembered James 2:15-16 where it states that sometimes it's not good enough to only pray for someone. Instead, we needed to be more specific in our giving that evening. It would require both prayer and financial contributions to help LifeGuard pay off the debt. Then Psalm 24:1 reminded me that everything belongs to our Lord including our money.

"OK," I thought to myself, "Here's an opportunity to help reduce the number of abortions and at the same time, be able to participate in a Christ-centered movie." This was a win win situation. I then thought about my sister who was going through a rough time. "If only I could get her involved with this," I thought. She is a big fan of Metanoia films that created "*Bella*." I had a split second opportunity to help make my sister's dreams come true by providing her and her family with the opportunity to be in a movie with the filmmakers she so admired.

Just before I was ready to commit, it suddenly dawned on me that the next day my wife had planned on ordering some long- awaited furniture she had been saving up for. I thought, "How could we afford both?" Ironically, the cost of the furniture just happened to be the exact price needed to bid for the donation and film opportunity. When I brought this up to my wife, she quickly put her hands to her mouth and started laughing. It was so contagious that I nearly lost it as well. After she calmed down, I asked her if she would be willing to give up the furniture. Without hesitation, she replied, "It's only furniture, besides how much better spent could our money be than on something like this." I said, "Are you sure?" She just nodded her head in agreement. I told her that I would agree if my sister and her family could also be included.

My wife went up to the producer and told him what we had been discussing and he immediately agreed to everything. I had already walked outside for some fresh air (to hide) so she came running after me to tell me the good news. All I could think about was how happy this would make my son and sister when they found out. After thanking the producer for his generosity toward us and LifeGuard, I immediately called my sister and told her that she was going to Hollywood. Of course, she thought I was joking until the producer who was still nearby asked for the phone to tell her in person. Talk about a dream come true! When he handed the phone back to me, my sister was laughing hysterically and when she heard my voice, her laughter intermixed with tears of joy. I have never heard her that excited before. It was worth ever penny of it just to hear her so happy.

This all happened at the right place, at the right time, with the right people. To cap it off, the producer asked that all the married couples come up and dance to one of the final slow songs played that night. He was insistent that all couples come up and that meant us. I hadn't been on a dance floor for 18 years since my wife and I got married, but there I was dancing with my wife, and I actually enjoyed it. Thank God for all He does for us even when we don't deserve it. And thank God for people like the producer and the rest of Metanoia Films for taking valuable time out of their lives to help those in need, especially the unborn. **(End of update)**

Financial Discipline

In order for us to be better stewards of our resources, we have to exercise restraint and manage God's financial gifts wisely. Living a simpler lifestyle will enable us to reduce our debt as much as possible and more importantly, will allow us to devote more time and effort to our relationship with Christ and others around us. Our Lord doesn't want us to become slaves to anything. (1 Corinthians 7:23), (Romans 13:8)

> *You were bought at a price; do not become slaves of men.*
>
> *Let no debt remain outstanding, except the continuing debt to love one another, for he who loves his fellowman has fulfilled the law.*

We would be a lot better off to follow the last Scripture "Let no debt remain outstanding . . . ." Unfortunately, this is not possible for most of us in our present generation who probably wouldn't be able to own a home, or for that matter, even an automobile if it weren't for credit. It's obvious that times have changed since this Scripture was written so we have to adjust accordingly, but need to recognize that the main message is still relevant to our present times.

Never before have there been so many choices – materialism is all around us and has a powerful influence over our lives. Since the advent of credit cards, it has become too convenient to purchase most anything, and finding a balance in this madness can be difficult. Once a product becomes popular with society most of us want it, and in some cases, will go into serious debt to get it. What we need and what we want are two different things that are commonly confused with one another. Obviously we need food and shelter to survive but what about the things that go beyond survival?

Where should Christians draw the line between simple enjoyment and obsession? Is a 32-inch LCD television large enough or do we need a 60-inch high definition flat screen before we can truly experience a program? There is nothing wrong with purchasing a 60-inch LCD as long as we can afford it and use it for God's glory. But do we really need the latest and greatest or could we settle for a little less, especially if it results in less debt?

Placing ourselves into debt for something that we really don't need is contrary to Scripture, especially if the newly acquired debt places a burden on our finances. God does not want us to be in bondage to lifeless material objects. Unfortunately, this is exactly what has happened to a large number of Christians and has left some of us spending more time with our possessions than we do in prayer with our Lord. I know I'm guilty of this and need to get my priorities straight by focusing on what's really important.

Can you imagine God's perspective on this material madness? Ancient Israel had a few idols in their darkest times and we have our millions! Our obsession with material objects has made some of us willing to risk our relationships with family, and even with God. Why do we place ourselves into financial bondage? Are these things really making us happy or are they causing undo financial stress that has led some of us to the brink of physical and spiritual bankruptcy? The more distractions we have, the less time we spend with God and our families. (Luke 16:13)

> No servant can serve two masters. Either he will hate the one and love the other, or he will be devoted to the one and despise the other. You cannot serve both God and money.

Jesus, while in Judean territory with his disciples, came upon a man that was very wealthy and claimed to be a true follower of God. (Matthew 19:16-22)

> *Now a man came up to Jesus and asked, "Teacher, what good thing must I do to get eternal life?"*
>
> *"Why do you ask me about what is good?" Jesus replied. "There is only One who is good. If you want to enter life, obey the commandments."*
>
> *"Which ones?" the man inquired.*
>
> *Jesus replied, " 'Do not murder, do not commit adultery, do not steal, do not give false testimony, honor your father and mother,' and 'love your neighbor as yourself.' "*
>
> *"All these I have kept," the young man said. "What do I still lack?"*
>
> *Jesus answered, "If you want to be perfect, go, sell your possessions and give to the poor, and you will have treasure in heaven. Then come, follow me." When the young man heard this, he went away sad, because he had great wealth.*

In His reply to the young man, I think Jesus was talking to all of us. Speaking on my own behalf, it would be extremely hard to give up everything. Regardless, His words should be taken seriously when evaluating our own priorities and how they affect our relationship with God. When we die, we will have to give up everything we own whether we want to or not. Only through prayer and self-sacrifice can we learn to put less emphasis on material things and more on what is really important – our relationship with Christ.

Trust in God

What if we are just trying to keep our heads above water and struggle financially on a day to day basis? Most of us, at some point in our lives, have gone through this burden and it is in times like these that I like to read my favorite Scripture: (Matthew 6:25-36).

> *"Therefore I tell you, do not worry about your life, what you will eat or drink; or about your body, what you will wear. Is not life more important than food, and the body more important than clothes? Look at the birds of the air; they do not sow or reap or store away in barns, and yet your heavenly Father feeds them. Are you not much more valuable than they? Who of you by worrying can add a single hour to his life?*
>
> *"And why do you worry about clothes? See how the lilies of the field grow. They do not labor or spin. Yet I tell you that not even Solomon in all his splendor was dressed like one of these. If that is how God clothes the grass of the field, which is here today and tomorrow is thrown into the fire, will he not much more clothe you, O you of little faith? So do not worry, saying, 'What shall we eat?' or 'What shall we drink?' or 'What shall we wear?' For the pagans run after all these things, and your heavenly Father knows that you need them. But seek first his kingdom and his righteousness, and all these things will be given to you as well. Therefore do not worry about tomorrow, for tomorrow will worry about itself. Each day has enough trouble of its own.*

If we trust these words and put Christ first, we will spend less time worrying and more time enjoying our lives because we will know that Jesus is looking out for us and will never abandon us. This is a comforting thought when trouble comes our way. It is extremely stressful to be short on money and is definitely one of the more difficult challenges we face. In the end, it all comes down to faith – do we really believe there is a loving God who looks after our every need? And if we believe, do we trust Him to help us?

† † †

Back when my brother and I first started college, we worked for my dad's commercial construction business to earn extra money for tuition. His business was going through an unusually slow period and it was putting our whole family in financial jeopardy. My brother and I realized the seriousness of the situation so we decided to act on God's promise for tithing and gave one hundred dollars of our quickly disappearing money to a charitable mission located in the Eastern United States. We received a letter that looked like all the other junk mail but for some reason it stood out. Their plea for help to fund a school that supported Native Americans made an impact on us. Our family has a special place in our hearts for Native Americans because Mom and Dad lived on the Navajo Reservation for a year, early in their marriage. This was also where my brother was born.

No more than a few hours after mailing the money off, I ran into an old friend I hadn't seen in several years. We did some catching up and I found out that he was working for his dad who was also a general contractor. Come to find out, they were in need of someone to do all the foundation work for a large church job they had recently been awarded and needed to start right away. Later that evening while eating dinner, my brother and I explained to the rest of our family what had happened, and for good reason, Dad in particular seemed interested in our account. Within a matter of weeks, we were awarded the contract. God honored our charitable gift by blessing our family financially, but more importantly, I can now see how God was planting seeds of faith that would bear fruit in all of us and would become especially fruitful in my dad's later conversion.

Making a living can be very hard at times. It presents us with difficult challenges that can either be brought on by our own actions or by circumstances beyond our control. We may not be able to avoid the unknown, but we can do something about the problems that we get ourselves into. In other words, we need to do whatever is necessary to free ourselves and our loved ones from unnecessary debt. If selling a larger home and moving into a smaller, more affordable one eases the burden then we need to do it. We have to ask ourselves what is more important, a larger home or the well being of our family? I know this option is not always possible for some, but for others where it is, every effort should be made to ensure we provide the best possible Christian environment for our families, both physically and spiritually.

This is all easier said than done considering the fact that we live in a society where the cost of living has become extremely expensive. This places a lot of undue stress on our families. In many cases, it requires both parents to hold down jobs even if mom would rather stay home with the children. For some of us it may seem impossible at times to balance out our Christian duties with our financial obligations. But if we really want to honor and obey our Lord, He will find a way for us. (Luke 18:27)

> Jesus replied, "What is impossible with men is possible with God."

Some of us struggle just to meet the bare necessities and others have more than they need; however, each can have happiness if we trust in God and are thankful for what we have. Lasting joy can only come from Him – not through the present circumstances in our lives. God will level out the playing field because He has no favorites and loves all of us equally. (Acts 10:34)

> Then Peter began to speak: "I now realize how true it is that God does not show favoritism."

Some receive the blessing of financial wealth and have the ability to give their money generously to others who are less fortunate. Others are blessed with time and talent which enables them to help out in a hands-on, more personal way. Another person has the gift of compassion and is able to comfort those in need. Someone else has the ability to make people laugh even when they are going through a difficult time. The list goes on and on. We are all blessed with unique qualities that help us glorify our Lord.

A person with great financial wealth that is diagnosed with a deadly disease would likely trade a poor person for their good health. Yet a poor person who is healthy may dream of being rich some day, ignoring their blessing of good health. Nothing is wrong with wanting to have both wealth and health as long as we don't take what we have for granted, and more importantly, we keep our eyes focused on Christ. We often hear the expression, "At least you still have your health." This is an understatement because without it, especially our spiritual health, everything else doesn't really matter. We should thank God every day for this wonderful blessing.

Pilgrimage to Israel

As a child, I use to think that rich people couldn't get into Heaven after hearing the following Scripture found in Matthew 19:23-26:

> *Then Jesus said to his disciples, "I tell you the truth, it is hard for a rich man to enter the kingdom of heaven. Again I tell you, it is easier for a camel to go through the eye of a needle than for a rich man to enter the kingdom of God."*
>
> *When the disciples heard this, they were greatly astonished and asked, "Who then can be saved?" Jesus looked at them and said, "With man this is impossible, but with God all things are possible."*

It took a trip across the Atlantic Ocean all the way to the Holy Land to finally learn the true meaning of this Scripture.

When my wife and I were first married we had the wonderful opportunity to visit Israel while on our honeymoon. My sister's friend set us up with a recently widowed Jewish woman who had an organization that supported Jews that believed in Jesus. She needed someone to help build an addition to expand her ministry. We volunteered to help out but when we arrived, the project had been canceled. Instead, she welcomed us to stay in her home. We didn't feel comfortable accepting her generous invitation with the remodel canceled, but her insistence won out. In order to show her appreciation for our willingness to help out, she personally assigned two of her new tour guides to show us around Israel. They were a married couple in training and we were their first customers. Overwhelmed by her generosity, we insisted that we do something in exchange. We came to a mutual agreement. My wife and I would work on repairing her house in between our travels with the tour guides. This went on for two weeks and we had the time of our lives!

On one of our trips while visiting the old city of Jerusalem, we came upon one of the large gates to the city that had a smaller gate built into its bottom center. It was brought to our attention by a local historian that opening the main gate would leave the city vulnerable to an attack from their enemies, so a smaller gate was made. This was just large enough for a camel, with all of its contents taken off its back, to get down on its knees and literally crawl through it. Access was difficult but not impossible. Our tour guides went on to say that just as the camel had to get on its knees and strip all its possessions, so does the rich person to enter the kingdom of Heaven. This brought a whole new meaning to the Scripture and I quickly learned from my experiences in Israel that we need a better understanding of Jewish culture in order to more fully understand and appreciate the real meaning of the Bible.

We also had the opportunity to travel to Masada, where King Herod built a beautiful palace on the edge of a massive cliff, towering high above the Dead Sea. During the Roman siege of Israel in 70 A.D., a group of Jewish zealots embarrassed Rome by taking control of this impenetrable fortress. During this time period, it became one of the last Jewish strong holds before the Romans completely conquered them.

Shortly after arriving there, we took the gondola to the top of this historic mountain. We wanted to hike up the steep trail, but due to the blistering 106-degree heat, we chose the alternative. As we gained elevation, the views of the Dead Sea and surrounding landscapes became more incredible. Near the top, a large flock of brilliant white pelicans were taking advantage of the rising, hot desert air in order to gain elevation on their southern journey to Africa. Reaching the top, it quickly became evident how only a handful of Jewish people could fend off a large Roman army for such a long period of time. In order to overcome this impenetrable mountain, the Romans had to build an earthen ramp of epic proportions all the way to its summit. Though it was an incredible sight to see, an eerie feeling came upon me when I realized how many Jewish slaves must have been killed in the process of building this ramp.

Our guides informed us that after Israel became a nation in 1948, their military was the first to uncover the ruins of Masada and they determined that all had committed suicide rather than be captured by the Romans. In the ruins, they found ancient prophesy inscribed on stone walls that foretold God's promise that He would once again rebuild their nation and by reading this, prophesy was being fulfilled. Standing there on the actual site hearing this incredible account was a powerful, moving experience.

When it was time to leave this historic site, my wife and I decided to forgo the gondola and hike down the steep trail despite the intense heat. Never before have we experienced such profuse sweating and after reaching the bottom, we were exhausted and in need of some cold water. Our guides said they knew just the place to get refreshed a few miles up the road along the Dead Sea coast. Little did we know that they were taking us to the Springs of En Gedi where David hid out from King Saul. We came to a parking lot and I noticed a trail leading up a narrow, cliff-bound canyon full of vegetation with a stream running through it. Despite being tired, we couldn't wait to hike up the trail to discover a new adventure. Within minutes, we came to a waterfall that emptied into a deep pool of clear cold water. It was a spectacular setting and we didn't waste any time jumping in – what a welcome relief from the heat!

The whole scene was like a dream and it made me realize why King David was so inspired when writing some of the Psalms here. We met an Arab and a Jewish family vacationing there and it was comforting to see them both peacefully enjoying the same pool of water together. Their friendly co-existence was not an isolated incident and we saw this happening on numerous occasions while traveling.

In between our travels throughout the Holy Land, we tore out our host's marble countertops and rebuilt the supporting wood framework that had deteriorated from water damage. We also replaced aged plumbing parts and worked on anything else that was in need of repair. The working part of our trip was just as enjoyable as the traveling – getting to know and help out the local people and their families was a very rewarding experience. I can still remember the delicious taste of a falafel burger that was offered to us by a local vendor. We were blessed to have our own personal tour guides and our experience will never be forgotten. I hope and pray that her ministry is alive and well and I thank God for our unique adventure.

We visited other beautiful locations too numerous to mention, but more importantly, we walked in the footsteps of Jesus. The drama of His life became more real, instilling a faith within us that would not have been possible without this experience.

My wife and I were visiting Israel not too long after the walls of communism in the former Soviet Union came falling down. Because of this historic event, we were able to witness first hand, planes filled with Jewish immigrants from the former Soviet Union and Africa being set free from years of persecution. As they got off the planes, most of them kissed the ground and lifted their hands towards Heaven, openly praising God for their good fortune. It was an event that brought tears to my eyes and shivers throughout my body – we were witnessing prophesy being fulfilled right before our eyes!

This prophetic event was foretold long ago in the following Scripture. (Isaiah, 43: 5-7)

> *Do not be afraid, for I am with you; I will bring your children from the East and gather you from the West.*
>
> *I will say to the north, 'Give them up!' and to the South, 'do not hold them back.' Bring my sons from afar and my daughters from the ends of the earth – everyone who is called by my name, who I created for my glory, who I formed and made.*

God really does live up to his promises and to actually witness it being realized was a life changing event.

Russian Coup

On our trip to and from Israel, we had a stop over in Sofia, Bulgaria, a former communist country hardened by decades of oppressive rule. Sofia had recently been liberated from the former Soviet Union and we had the unique opportunity to witness this first hand during our two layovers there. On our first stop, we had several hours to go into the city and explore this once hidden culture. When we got off the jet, we must have stuck out like a sore thumb because we were instantly surrounded by taxicab drivers and other vendors competing for our business. We quickly got the impression that they thought we were rich because we were American. Hollywood's long arm had portrayed the false image that most everyone living in our country was wealthy with large homes and fancy cars. This couldn't be further from the truth. We are, however, blessed in America with a wonderful constitution that affords us religious freedom which some of these people living in Sofia literally died for while under communist rule.

I had this same experience while traveling with my sister in the former Yugoslavia, (now Croatia) a few years before. When my sister and I got off the plane in Dubrovnik, I was surrounded by a dozen older Croatian women who literally tugged at my shirt from all directions. I found out they were competing with one another for the right to have us stay at their home with the anticipation of being paid a handsome wage for their hospitality. This included home cooked meals and a small room to sleep in. Twenty dollars per night was cheap for us but was a treasure for them. Dubrovnik was one of the most beautiful cities I've ever seen. Its placement along the shores of the aqua-blue Adriatic Sea with its medieval castles and white stucco buildings was almost too beautiful to behold. We just couldn't take in enough of it. We traveled up the coast and into the interior on a journey of faith that will never be forgotten. Unfortunately, shortly after we left, the whole country broke out into a horrible civil war that divided Yugoslavia into several different countries.

Sofia, Bulgaria, couldn't compare to the beauty of Dubrovnik although each area has its own unique qualities if you take the time to look for them. My wife and I were surprised by the number of American flags the citizens of Sofia had imprinted on their clothing and posted on numerous walls throughout their city. We caught a cab into the main city square which was surrounded by a large park with older, monochromatic-looking high rise apartment buildings at its perimeter. On the way there we noticed that the few gas stations available, had lineups at least a city block long. The highway itself had little traffic and it seemed somewhat desolate.

However, at the city park there were people walking everywhere. We sat down on a bench where some older men were playing cards and I asked them what they did for work in Sofia. At first, they just stared at me and finally one of them asked what we were doing there. They acted as if they hadn't seen too many tourists over the years. I told them our story which loosened them up a bit and they went on to explain how hard it was to get consistent work. In the middle of the park was a bronze statue of one of their former leaders. I think it was Stalin. That day, the sky was a gloomy grey which was the way I had envisioned a former Soviet Republic to look like. As we walked around the park, people mostly stared at us and didn't seem overly friendly despite all their American flag paraphernalia. We didn't take it personal because we knew that Americans probably didn't travel there very often, especially when Bulgaria was under communist rule.

† † †

On the way back from Israel, our plane once again stopped over in Sofia, but this time things had changed for the worse. We had arrived in the middle of the Russian Coup attempt in August 1991. The hard line communists tried once again to overtake their former republics, but in the end the will of the people triumphed. After returning home, I can still remember the news scenes of the mass demonstrations of people surrounding Russian tanks which concluded with the army siding with them, quickly ending the brief coup attempt.

As our jet came in for its final approach to Sofia, I noticed that the shared military/public airport had an increased presence of artillery and planes on the ground. When our plane came to a stop on the tarmac, the ground crew immediately opened up the cargo hatch and literally started throwing the passengers' luggage out in a big pile onto the concrete. The same thing happened on the first trip here but the workers were more careful and organized.

This time we could tell things had changed. We got off the plane and went over to the pile to claim our luggage and noticed that a man was walking off with one of our bags. I ran up and politely informed him that the bag he was carrying belonged to us and he just stared at me for a brief moment and handed it over without incident. Entering the airport building, there was a crowd of passengers from different parts of Europe and there seemed to be a lot of confusion. We were then rudely instructed to get into a line that led to customs.

On our first trip through, they did not require a fee for our visas but now, because of the coup, they were requiring that my wife who was a Canadian citizen, to pay $20. She was upset because they didn't require me to pay anything because I was American. She asked them why she was being discriminated against but they didn't give her an answer. Then they escorted her into a separate room and when I tried to follow, a man blocked my access and told me I couldn't go in with her so I begrudgingly waited in the lobby. I could tell that the communists had briefly taken power again by their mean spirited, controlling attitudes. It made me extremely uncomfortable to let her out of my sight but I didn't have a choice. The room she went into was separated from the rest of the lobby by an eight-foot tall wall divider with no attached ceiling above them. As I sat there waiting for her to come out, horrible thoughts kept going through my mind. I kept thinking of Richard Wurmbrand who was tortured by communists in Romania because of his faith. I had also read that hundreds of Christians, Turks, and Jews were tortured in Bulgaria while under the control of the former Soviet Union.

After she didn't come out for several minutes, I couldn't take it any longer and jumped up on a desk that enabled me to reach the top of the wall that separated me from my wife. I then climbed over the top and jumped to the floor where I remained undetected. I could see her standing at the opposite corner of the room and she appeared to be doing ok. As I started walking towards her, I was finally detected by the same man that wouldn't let me in before. He quickly grabbed my arm and loudly asked how I had gotten in there and told me that I would have to leave immediately. By this time my adrenaline was pumping and I shook free from his grip and told him that I was just looking for my wife but would leave as he insisted. Just knowing that she was alright was enough to allow me to regain my composure, and thankfully, I went back to the lobby without incident.

My wife wasn't aware of what had just transpired as she waited in line to pay for her visa. She became further upset when they raised her original quote of $20 to $40. When she finally came back into the lobby, she complained to me about what had transpired. I told her that I risked being thrown in jail to ensure her safety and all she could think about was the extra money. We both just laughed! Soon afterwards, we were literally herded into a large room which was packed full with people. There were kids crying and people were loudly talking in various languages which created an atmosphere of mass confusion. It was also extremely hot with no apparent ventilation which is one of my worst nightmares. Then over the loud speaker, it was announced that all flights had been cancelled until further notice.

There we were, trapped in a hot stuffy room, and now our flight had been cancelled. To make matters worse, someone in the room threw up causing a severe stench that started a chain reaction of people losing their lunch. It was more than I could handle and I started looking for a way out. To our relief, they finally opened the doors to the main airport lobby which literally saved my sanity. We went to the counter to ask what was going on and they informed us that none of their planes would be able to fly out because of unusual circumstances beyond their control.

To give you a little history, my sister was a travel agent at the time and I asked her to find us the cheapest flight possible to Israel. She took me at my word and found a new, reasonably priced airline. They had recently purchased several new Airbus jets and their operations were located in Bulgaria. Here was a former communist country reaching out into the free market world and we were some of their first customers. Unfortunately for us, we were at the wrong place at the wrong time. It wasn't the airline's fault. Their service was pretty good with the exception of opening the shades to our window to wake us up in the middle of our transcontinental flight, insisting that we eat our scheduled breakfast at that moment. They were still getting used to customer service. On our trip overseas, they had an unannounced stopover in Ottawa, Canada, which surprised everyone onboard. My wife was happy because it was the first time see had been to her capital.

It was the Bulgarian government that had forced them to shut down because of the coup attempt that was now in progress. They told us it could be several days before we would be able to leave. This was not what we wanted hear. After sweating it out for several hours, we received some excellent news. The airline had worked out a deal with Swiss Air to bring planes in to help out with the crisis. Within a few hours the planes arrived, and what a beautiful sight it was. Swiss Air has one of the best reputations in the industry. We were greeted by extremely kind stewardesses before entering the plane – I felt like I was going to Heaven. After boarding, they announced that we would be flown straight to Zurich, Switzerland, and would be provided with a complimentary suite and dinner for the night before continuing our flight to the US the next day.

This was like a dream come true. We went from an extremely uncomfortable and scary situation to one of complete bliss in a matter of hours. The overnight stay in Zurich was wonderful and the next day they flew us home in a beautiful 747. The Bulgarian airline should take most of the credit for doing such an excellent job in taking care of their customers.

I brought this story up because it gave us just a tiny glimpse of what people behind the Iron Curtain, including the newly freed Jewish people, had to go through on a regular basis. I remember how good it felt to get out of our own dilemma and it gave us a slight perspective of how the Jewish immigrants must have felt after suffering great hardships for many years and finally being able to return to their promised land. Praise God for He is good!

Treasure in Heaven

We are blessed to live in such a prosperous nation and after traveling abroad, I realized how fortunate I was to be born in this country. However, we can all learn a lot from other cultures, especially those who are family-oriented and live a simple way of life.

Even with our God-given prosperity, it is still important that we are generous and responsible with our finances and should never extend ourselves above our means. Financial responsibility includes the present as well as the future. As important as saving for the future is, it is unfortunate we can spend most of our lives planning for our earthly retirement and not enough on the eternal – it lasts much longer and should be the main purpose for our lives. Jesus tells us to store up treasure in Heaven because He knows first hand how wonderful it is and deeply desires that everyone share it with Him.

Our brief time on Earth has eternal consequences; therefore, it is the most important period of our existence. Our decisions in this world will dictate where we will spend eternity. This also holds true with our finances, so before investing in anything large or small, we have a moral obligation to make sure our investments are free from anything contrary to Scripture. We also have to realize that we are not alone when dealing with our finances; rather, we have a wonderful loving God that looks after our every need and He will never abandon us no matter how desperate or prosperous our situation becomes.

Whether we are struggling financially or have more than we know what to do with, God loves us all and wants each of us to enjoy our lives to the fullest. There is nothing wrong with having goals for a better financial future as long as these goals do not interfere with our commitment to God, family, and others around us.

I will conclude this chapter with the following Scripture. (1 Timothy 6:6-19)

> *But Godliness with contentment is great gain. For we brought nothing into the world, and we can take nothing out of it. But if we have food and clothing, we will be content with that. People who want to get rich fall into temptation and a trap and into many foolish and harmful desires that plunge men into ruin and destruction. For the love of money is a root of all kinds of evil. Some people, eager for money, have wandered from the faith and pierced themselves with many griefs.*
>
> *But you, man of God, flee from all this, and pursue righteousness, godliness, faith, love, endurance and gentleness. Fight the good fight of the faith. Take hold of the eternal life to which you were called when you made your good confession in the presence of many witnesses. In the sight of God, who gives life to everything, and of Christ Jesus, who while testifying before Pontius Pilate made the good confession, I charge you to keep this command without spot or blame until the appearing of our Lord Jesus Christ, which God will bring about in his own time—God, the blessed and only Ruler, the King of kings and Lord of lords, who alone is immortal and who lives in unapproachable light, whom no one has seen or can see. To him be honor and might forever. Amen.*
>
> *Command those who are rich in this present world not to be arrogant nor to put their hope in wealth, which is so uncertain, but to put their hope in God, who richly provides us with everything for our*

enjoyment. Command them to do good, to be rich in good deeds, and to be generous and willing to share. In this way they will lay up treasure for themselves as a firm foundation for the coming age, so that they may take hold of the life that is truly life.

Update – May 2, 2009

I wrote this chapter on debt and materialism back in late 2006. Little did I know how quickly our problem with debt would force us into a worldwide recession. It all came on so suddenly, catching almost everyone by surprise. The partial sentence in the above Scripture, ". . . Neither to put their hope in the uncertainty of wealth but in God," really strikes home in our present financial crisis. I will go over this in further detail in chapter 9.

Chapter 5

Obedience to Godly Principles

Just like with everything else in life there are rules and living a Christian life is no exception. Through the Bible, God has given us a road map to follow, and if we already have a map that gives us clear direction, why is there so much controversy amongst Christians? I can understand why religion is controversial among different faiths, but what about people with the same beliefs? Isn't the Bible clear on core issues and doesn't it give us clear instructions on how to live our lives? At least part of the reason is fairly clear – we tend to pick and choose what we want to believe and discard the rest. If Scripture interferes with our lifestyle, we sometimes rationalize and manipulate it to suit our own particular needs.

Peer Pressure

Is it impossible to live a true Christian life in today's secular world, especially when dealing with our younger generation? My son has felt this pressure first hand while playing baseball. He is also one of the few players that isn't hooked on chewing tobacco which drives some of the other kids crazy. On bus trips to away games he is constantly pressured to try it. On one trip, a player asked him in front of several other teammates if the reason why he didn't chew was because he was a Christian. My son just smiled and replied by nodding yes. Immediately afterward with a big chew in the side of his mouth, the boy asking the question sarcastically claimed that he was also a Christian. My son just laughed and exclaimed, "No you're not," and the boy smiled back and said, "You're right, I'm not." A few moments later, he became really quiet and my son noticed his face had turned bright red and that he was having a difficult time breathing. He then began choking violently and started throwing up all over the bus. Sitting next to him, my son barely had enough time to hop over the bus seat nearly missing the shower of vomit. Most of the kids in the bus started laughing at him saying, "You can't handle your chew!" The boy was extremely embarrassed and remained quiet the rest of the trip.

It was as if God allowed this to happen to teach him a lesson for trying to pressure my son into doing it and to give that boy a bad experience chewing so he might think twice about doing it again. The second lesson wasn't learned but he did stop trying to pressure my son. Some of the boys addicted to chew were also getting into alcohol and even drugs.

The need to be accepted by our peers is a powerful force. At first it is all fun and games, but if those boys only knew how addictive nicotine and other drugs and alcohol were, they might think twice before becoming hooked on these dangerous, life threatening substances. Why are we so addicted to things that are bad for us and why do we think bad things are so cool? The boys in this story are good kids and I have personally known some of them since their early youth. I hate to see them become addicted but feel there is little I can do to stop them – it's frustrating to say the least. Unfortunately, most of us are rebellious by nature and without God in our lives, most of us do not stand a chance.

My sister's oldest son is in high school and has had kids offer to pay him to say the "F" word. They can't understand why he won't say it. I know for a fact that deep down, kids and adults actually respect others for maintaining a moral conduct. I constantly had students at my high school asking me why I didn't do drugs and I simply told them that I didn't want or need to. Most of them respected my answer but occasionally I would get harassed over it.

While at a party, someone would offer me a beer, but before I could say no, friends around me would tell them I don't drink, almost as if they were my own personal guardians. This went on for a few years but then something happened to change all of that.

I thought I was invincible until I made a bad decision by slowly playing around with alcohol which quickly got out of control. Then I developed a relationship with a girl that only compounded the situation. Before I knew it, my life was quickly getting out of control. I knew I had a problem because I couldn't stop drinking with just a couple of beers. Instead, I would keep drinking until I blacked out. This was the most vulnerable period of my life. My friends claimed that I ran across a busy six-lane highway with cars forced to slam on their brakes to avoid hitting me. How I wasn't killed was a miracle. The next day I couldn't remember anything about the night before. I was told that I once went up to a big football player's girlfriend and start hugging her right in front of him. Lucky for me, he just laughed at my miserable condition and didn't pound me into the ground.

I remember my homecoming dance where I became so intoxicated that I was falling all over the place while trying to dance with my girlfriend. One of my teachers noticed my behavior and booted me out the door into the cool fall night. My girlfriend escorted me to my truck where she left me alone in my misery. Lying on the floor board on the verge of passing out, I briefly remember throwing my guts out, feeling like I was going to die. I pleaded with God to save me and told Him if He would stop the pain, I wouldn't drink again. I don't even remember how I got home that night.

I was such a hypocrite because I used to make fun of some of my friends when they made a fool out of themselves while drinking.

On one such occasion, some friends and I were at a party and we were tossing a tennis ball around in a basement. One of my friends had too much to drink and tried to take the ball away from me. I barely pushed him and he tumbled into a pan of used motor oil. Drenched with oil, he started chasing me but I easily avoided his grasp. He then went up stairs to where most of the people were and started grabbing a hold of them to help maintain his balance, smearing oil on everyone he touched. One guy didn't appreciate it so he shoved him into a wall which dislodged a structure holding dozens of plants. They all came crashing to the ground, breaking pottery and spewing plants and soil all over the living room floor. I was told later that several football players got a hold of him and threw him out the door into a snowdrift on a very cold winter night.

At the time, I wasn't aware they had thrown him outside. When we decided to leave, a friend and I saw what appeared to be a body lying face first in the snow. Going over for a closer look, I realized who it was. My friend's face was purple and he was literally freezing to death. He had been out there for at least an hour with the temperature in the low teens. We pulled him out of the snow and after shaking him repeatedly, he finally opened his eyes. We drove him home and let his mom take care of the rest. I remember thinking to myself that I would never get myself into that kind of situation, but there I was, doing things even more foolish.

That is why it is so important to stay away from drinking and drug parties or any other activity that can get us into trouble. We may be able to resist these temptations for a while but all it takes is one vulnerable period in our life to suck us in as it did in mine. The best way to stay clear from trouble is to avoid it all together.

God has warned us to stay away from all tempting situations to avoid falling into sin. I had to learn the hard way and am very fortunate to be living today. Through God's mercy, I was able to snap out of my addiction to alcohol before it became a lifetime curse. My drinking binge lasted for over a year and nearly cost me my life. Alcohol addiction runs in my family and I knew I would be better off if I didn't drink at all. There is nothing wrong with a glass of wine or a beer with dinner when at a legal drinking age, but if you're like me, you are better off quitting altogether. I haven't missed it at all and thank Jesus for helping me stop before it killed me or even worse, someone else. Addictions require supernatural intervention to end them and only through Christ can we avoid these vices that separate us from Him.

You may be made fun of temporarily if you say no to drugs and alcohol, but if you persevere, others will actually respect and envy you for your convictions. Most importantly, you will be a good example for others to follow. Deep down, people know the truth, and when they see it in action they too will be drawn to follow our Lord's example.

Premarital Sex

Premarital sex can be as addictive as drugs or alcohol and can be just as dangerous to our health and soul. I know first hand that it is difficult to date someone for a long period of time and remain celibate. Not only can it result in pregnancy or a sexually transmitted disease, it will leave you feeling guilty, empty, insecure, and ultimately, it can destroy your relationship with the other person and with Christ.

God created sex to be fulfilling only between a husband and wife. Anything outside of marriage will only lead to despair. Leaving yourself pure for your future spouse is the ultimate gift to them and more importantly, it is pleasing to God. Discipline, commitment, prayer, and obedience to God are absolutely necessary to avoid this type of sin. We should abstain from this type of behavior not just to prevent disease or avoid pregnancy, but primarily because we love God and do not want to sin against Him or our own bodies. God doesn't give us rules to punish us; rather, it is for our own good – He knows what is best for us. (1 Corinthians 6:18-20, 7:8,9)

Flee from sexual immorality. All other sins a man commits are outside his body, but he who sins sexually sins against his own body. Do you not know that your body is a temple of the Holy Spirit, who is in you, whom you have received from God? You are not your own; you were bought at a price. Therefore honor God with your body.

Now to the unmarried and the widows I say: It is good for them to stay unmarried, as I am. But if they cannot control themselves, they should marry, for it is better to marry than to burn with passion.

I made the mistake of letting one of my relationships get too serious which caused me to abandon my friends and even quit the track and field team. When my coach found out, he was furious. He called me into his office and tried to knock some sense into my head but I didn't listen. I can still hear his words when he told me that I would look back one day and regret what I had done. When he saw that I wasn't responding, he grabbed my shirt collar and pushed me up against a wall and threatened to punch my lights out. He claimed the only thing holding him back was the threat of being fired. Looking back, I wish he would have knocked some sense into me – it would have saved a lot of heartache.

While a teenager, it is always better to keep the relationship on a plutonic basis. You will have a lot more fun that way and it will keep you out of a lot of potential trouble. It is far too easy to mistake hormonal passion with true love. Our youthful years only last for a brief period time and getting bogged down in a serious relationship is the last thing we should get into. It will consume most of your time and most often lead to failure. God is the only one that can permanently satisfy our hearts. That is why there is such a great need for Godly youth to live a Christian example for others in need to follow. However, if we claim to be Christian but do not follow Christ's teachings, we will fall into the same problems as the secular world.

Isn't God Always Right?

If we know God is extremely powerful and can overcome anything we face, then how can we justify our disobedient behavior? Isn't God always right or do we know better? I don't think most of us deliberately challenge God's Word; instead, we can become brainwashed by the culture we live in. Secular society is constantly telling us something contrary to Scripture which slowly but surely chips away at our faith. This cloud of corruption covers the truth of God's Word and we begin to feel comfortable modifying Scripture to suit our own needs. We need to wake up and look at this at face value – God is always right and we are always wrong when we act contrary to His Word. God gave us a free will to either choose His ways or follow our own modified path. However, He did not exempt us from the consequences of our decisions. Every choice we make has present and future implications for us personally and for those around us. Our actions literally influence the course of history. Our Lord mercifully holds all of us accountable for the choices we make.

If a person has too much alcohol to drink and makes the decision to drive impaired, immediate consequences can result. If while driving home, a person under the influence fails to stop at a red light resulting in the death of an innocent bystander, not only do we have the tragic loss of life, we also have whole generations of potential families lost by one person's poor decision.

Accepting Those Left Out

How many times have we been at a gathering where everyone else is busy socializing with each other and we notice a person sitting by themselves with no one to talk to? I know exactly how it feels to be in this awkward situation. I have been that isolated person on many occasions. People in general only want to talk to others they're familiar with and Christians are no exception to this rule. God, however, has called us to a higher standard and wants us to get out of our comfort zone and keep a constant eye out for those in need. We see this happen even in our churches. There is always that shy person, family, or couple standing there by themselves because no one has made them feel welcome. God is clear about us only showing love to those who love us. (Matthew 5:46-48)

> *If you love those who love you, what reward will you get? Are not even the tax collectors doing that? And if you greet only your brothers, what are you doing more than others? Do not even pagans do that? Be perfect, therefore, as your heavenly Father is perfect.*

To remain obedient to God, we have to reach out to those who are rejected by the world – the mentally ill, the homeless, the poor, the sick, the unlovable, etc. Training ourselves to be more conscious to the needs of others is absolutely necessary in becoming a better Christian. This in turn will enable us to be more successful in our relationship with God and with others around us. (James 2:1-4)

> *My brothers, as believers in our glorious Lord Jesus Christ, don't show favoritism. Suppose a man comes into your meeting wearing a gold ring and fine clothes, and a poor man in shabby clothes also comes in. If you show special attention to the man wearing fine clothes and say, "Here's a good seat for you," but say to the poor man, "You stand there" or "Sit on the floor by my feet," have you not discriminated among yourselves and become judges with evil thoughts?*

When I was in junior high school, I was known as the "pinhead bodyguard." If someone tried to bully one of them, they knew they would have to answer to me. I wasn't able to stop them all, but to say the least I got along really well with the nerds. I have always had a place in my heart for the underdog – maybe because there have been times in my life when I was/am included in this category. Because of this, I know how it feels to be left out. It is a very painful, gut-wrenching experience that can cause great harm to your self-esteem. My son can't figure out why I usually side with the underdog while watching sports instead of rooting for the favored team or player. When his favorite team loses he takes it so personal, as if he had lost himself. Especially at his age, most want to be associated with a winner because it makes us feel better about ourselves. This is only human nature and is why it is so hard to overcome our partiality towards others. Putting aside our biases can be difficult, but as Christians, we are commissioned with a fulltime endeavor to be fair and compassionate to one another. This requires plenty of prayer, commitment, and help from our Lord.

Hungry Stranger

After finishing up a job at our family's commercial retail building (on the lot that Grandpa got for free), I was sitting in my truck going over some paper work when I suddenly had a strange feeling that someone was watching me. I looked out my open window and was startled to see a man nicely dressed in western wear standing only a few feet away, staring at me. When he saw me flinch, he apologized for startling me and asked if I had any money he could borrow. I never expected that to come out of his mouth considering how well kept he looked. He didn't look like someone who needed money. He went on to tell me that he had recently lost his job in another state and was just passing through but had run out of money several days ago. He claimed he hadn't eaten a meal since.

As with most people, I never give money to anyone on the street because you never know whom you are dealing with and what they will use it for. The last thing a potential alcoholic or drug addict needs is money. I thought about it for a moment and told him I would be happy to buy him a meal at the fast food place across the street. I asked if he wouldn't mind walking over to the drive-up window where I would order and pay for his meal. He agreed so I drove over and placed the order. I doubled everything including desert.

When he saw that the order was ready, he eagerly came over to my truck and I handed it to him. With a quick thank you, he hurried over to a grassy area along the curb and started to devour his meal. He literally looked as if he was starving to death the way he was gobbling his food down. I stayed at the edge of the main road and watched him as long as I could before another car came up behind me which forced me to leave. At first it was almost funny watching him, but then my smile turned into tears. How could someone in our country become that bad off in such a short period of time? His clean appearance probably caused others to not take him seriously. I had to wonder how many people rejected his plea for help before I met up with him. Before I left, I told him where he could find a shelter and I could only hope that he listened to my advice.

I know if that were me, I would have had a hard time swallowing my pride. I learned first hand that it doesn't take very long for someone to become homeless. It could happen to almost anyone if they do not have family or friends to help them. To be left on your own, hungry and scared without a home, must be the worst feeling in the world. At the time, I wondered if the man was really an angel sent by our Lord to test me because he just didn't fit the bill of a homeless person. Today, however, I have seen this so many times that I realize this problem is real, especially in our present times.

Because of the dangerous world we live in, I wouldn't recommend that any woman or young man come in close contact with a stranger. I took precautions when helping the man by keeping him out of my truck. It is unfortunate that we can't all help out this way, but we never know whom we are dealing with and a person's safety has to be first on the list. I brought this up because this philosophy seems to put me at odds with the previous Scripture. However, we have to apply common sense when serving our Lord.

Abortion

The tragic decision to have an abortion, unless the life of the mother is truly in jeopardy, has immediate and long-term consequences. It's hard to comprehend the millions of aborted babies who never had the opportunity to live out their lives. It's even harder to believe that a civilized nation such as our own has allowed such a barbaric form of taking innocent life to be legalized, especially when it's used as a form of birth control. This is a perfect example of how a rationalizing mind can alter the truth and distort it to benefit their personal needs. The full weight of the sin resulting from the decision to choose an abortion does not lie only on the person making it. Society has allowed abortion to become legal and has even provided funding and the necessary facilities to make it more readily available.

Which is worse, a terrified young teenager's choice to have an abortion who may have been abandoned by her family, or a society that actually encourages young women to pursue this option? In my opinion, the latter is the worse sin and all of us participate in it in either a direct or indirect manner. When a person becomes frightened, they do things out of fear and desperation and may not even realize the consequences until it is too late. That is why it is so important that we have organizations such as local pregnancy centers, LifeGuard, Americans United For Life, National Right to Life, and all the others who are there to give women support in their time of need.

Some of us may ask the question, "How do I support abortion, I'm totally against it?" The most common way Christians support abortion is through the sin of omission – we complain but really don't do anything about it even though there are plenty of ways for us to help out. By comforting one in need, keeping an open line of communication with our children, participating in **nonviolent, peaceful** demonstrations, giving our time and money, writing our political leaders expressing our views against abortion, signing petitions, and most importantly, by praying and pleading with God that he will forgive us for this sin against humanity and will help us put an end to it.

In my opinion, the best way to end abortion is to reach deep into people's hearts out of love. The movie *Bella* is an excellent film that does a good job portraying the value of life through the examples of love, friendship, and family. It is a must see and is presented in such a way that everyone, including pro-choice advocates, can appreciate as well. http://www.metanoiafilms.com.

Voting

Political elections probably provide Christians with the best opportunity to help make a difference, not only with abortion, but with other problems that plague our society. Christians in particular, have a moral and civic responsibility to vote which allows us to publicly express our values and gives us the opportunity to help influence which leaders represent us in the local, state, and federal governments. Voting doesn't guarantee that we will get whom we want; rather, it allows us to make a public statement before God and society what we believe in, and that we are willing to make an effort to preserve these values.

We should never compromise our values just because a candidate doesn't belong to the same political party we do. Christians belong to God so we must follow His commandments no matter what the cost. Democrat, Republican, Independent, it doesn't matter when it comes down to principles – if a candidate supports abortion, how can a Christian justify voting for them? God is very clear about taking another's life, especially innocent life. In fact, this is one of the things that God hates the most. Proverbs 6:16-19 gives us a clear illustration of this.

> *There are six things the LORD hates, seven that are detestable to him:*
>
> *haughty eyes,*
>
> *a lying tongue,*
>
> *hands that shed innocent blood,*

a heart that devises wicked schemes, feet that are quick to rush into evil,

a false witness who pours out lies,

and a man who stirs up dissension among brothers.

Some situations are not so obvious especially when both candidates support anti-Christian views. I discussed this dilemma with a spiritual adviser and he told me to choose the lesser of two evils and pray about it. It may sound like the obvious thing to do but so many people stop voting because of this. A common expression is, "They're all corrupt and you can't believe anything they say so why bother voting?" This is a big mistake not only in the worldly sense, but more importantly in the spiritual. The sin of omission is a sin of inaction and if all Christians acted this way, elections would be left only to the secular world resulting in catastrophic consequences. Just because we vote for a particular candidate doesn't mean we're responsible for his or her actions – we voted for what was promised, not for what might actually happen. God looks at our hearts and is pleased when we bring ourselves to action to support his laws. There are many other social issues that need to be accounted for as well. The economy, health care, genetic research, education, national security, world events, and the judicial system are just a few of the complex issues that we face when voting.

God takes our voting records very seriously and one day we will have to give Him an account of our choices and I believe He will show us in full detail the consequences of our decisions. If we truly follow God's commandments and carefully choose leaders who best represent Christian values, we will be fulfilling Christ's will for us. This is essential in carrying out our Christian traditions and will help to ensure that they are successfully passed on to future generations. Our children are counting on us to make wise decisions.

Marriage and Family

"What about me?" has become a favorite expression used in today's selfish society. I have an easy time writing about this subject because I struggle with it on a daily basis. The attitude that we have the right to be happy is responsible for countless divorces and the break up of families. It is good to be happy as long as it doesn't come at the expense of others.

The choices we make in life can place us in stressful situations. Instead of blaming those around us, we need to be responsible for our own actions (easier said than done). Unfortunately, mothers and fathers are bailing out of their responsibilities of marriage at an alarming rate whenever things start getting tough. By giving up so easily, we are teaching our children that nothing is worth fighting for and nothing illustrates this better than through divorce. When mom or dad walks out the door, the affected children will never be the same. In some cases, divorce is the only option but too often it is the first choice without considering a more productive alternative. We have to remember that one kind compliment or a sincere apology can erase a truck load of problems in our marriage.

The Life Lessons of Baseball

As a baseball coach, I have seen this destructive "me first" attitude start at an early age. I have seen parents telling their ten-year-olds that being number one is all that matters. The parents carry the false hope that their kid will be playing professional sports making millions of dollars some day. For most, this couldn't be further from the truth. Instead of becoming a team player, the kid only focuses on their own performance at the expense of their teammates. If they make a mistake, they know that piercing scream coming from the bleachers is directed at them. I have seen this over and over again and have been guilty of it myself.

Bottom line, instead of us ruining their childhood, we need to encourage them to have fun and quit trying to live our lives and selfish dreams through them. For the most part, I have been fortunate to have such great parents to deal with. However, there have been a few occasions where a player has come up to me complaining about their dad. They claimed that as soon as he showed up, it would make them so nervous that they could hardly play the game. They went on to tell me that even if their dad wasn't yelling at them from the stands, they knew they would get the treatment on the way home. This was a wakeup call for me personally and I tried hard to make a concerted effort to not be that kind of dad even though on occasions, I have completely blown it. Baseball is supposed to be a positive time in their lives to enjoy, not dread – yet this is exactly what is happening too often.

Baseball is a life lesson because it teaches kids how to deal with other people. It is a team and individual sport all in one. If you want to be successful, you can't do it on your own. No matter how well you play as an individual, you still have to rely on your teammate's performance to ultimately win the game. This can help prepare them for marriage and other relationships in their lives.

Unfortunately, a few bad experiences from parents or a bad coach can discourage a kid from ever playing again. I'm not talking about the players who get chewed out because they are messing around too much and miss practices and then expect to play a lot in the following game. That's not how it works in baseball or in life. Those who put in more effort and discipline are usually rewarded more than those who don't. But for those players who are doing their part, it doesn't have to end in a bad way. One thing is for certain, as a coach, you will never make everyone happy, especially the players who sit on the bench more.

While coaching, I see bad habits getting players into serious slumps no matter what I tell them. "Jimmy, hold your bat back a little more and raise your hands a little higher." They try it one time and immediately say it doesn't feel right and go right back to their comfortably wrong swing. Their comfort zone is causing them to strike out at the plate but they insist it is the right swing for them. The older the player the harder it is to break the bad habit.

It is much easier to tell someone else how to break their bad habits than it is to change our own. When playing golf, I have a horrible slice to the right while using my driver. It seems no matter what I do to correct it, it doesn't get any better. My son has told me all along that my changes really aren't changes. I keep repeating the same wrong comfortable swing over and over again. He proved it to me by recording my swing on video and played it back for me in slow motion. Even after watching my ugly swing, I still couldn't make the necessary adjustments to correct it. Why is it so hard to change?

The same is true in our relationships with God and family. That is why it is so important to develop good habits of discipline, commitment, and love early in life before we get set in our stubborn ways. My mom and grandmother had every right in the world to divorce their husbands after putting up with their alcoholism for years. Both of them endured a lot of suffering by staying committed to their marriages even though at times, they probably should have left them, at least temporarily. Instead, through many hours of prayer, Mom and Grandma stuck it out even when others told them they were crazy to do so.

At one point when things were pretty bad, a friend asked Mom why she wouldn't get divorced. She explained her commitment to marriage but her friend just mocked her by claiming she was just too afraid to make the move. Her friend was probably right to some degree but Mom was a prayer warrior and that was the strength that kept her going.

Without God, I don't know how married couples can make it in our generation. It is a lot easier to cause problems for our spouse if we don't have a relationship with our Lord. With Him, He keeps us accountable for our actions by supernaturally convicting us in our sin. We may be able to hide things from our spouse, but as Christians, we know that our actions will not go unnoticed by God.

That is why it is so crucial to find someone who believes in Christ. However, just finding a Christian isn't enough; families and couples need to pray together on a regular basis if we expect God to heal our broken relationships and restore them to the holiness that He desires for all of us. It's all about prayer and commitment, capped off with patience and love.

Time is Short

Psalm 144:4

> *Man is like a breath; his days are like a fleeting shadow.*

Compared to eternal life, our time on Earth is flipping by like calendar pages in the wind, but this brief period of time is the most important in our existence – it has eternal consequences. We need to seize the moment by not wasting one precious second. We were placed on this Earth for one main purpose; God gave us a free will to choose Him and the choices we make will dictate where we spend eternity. As our own shadow quickly passes by, we must be careful not to get bogged down with our daily struggles. Instead, we must allow Jesus to lift us up above our problems so we can clearly see the path that leads to eternal life.

One trap we fall into is trying to accomplish too much in this life. We know that life is short and there is only so much time to accomplish our goals. If we're not careful, we can find ourselves jumping around never really accomplishing anything. We hear from others about their exotic trips overseas or about their latest adventure that seems too good to be true. This can make us feel like we are really missing out. Before we know it, we can become anxious and start planning things we really can't afford. The urge to live a little more usually gets worse with age and peaks during midlife – thus the term "midlife crisis." This can be a very challenging period in our lives. For some it can be quite humorous and remains innocent, but for others it can destroy entire families. Men and women, after being married for 20 plus years, will suddenly abandon their families by running off with another partner. This is happening at an alarming rate in today's society.

All this can be avoided if we will stay focused on God's Word and remember that our experiences in this life are not as important as in the one to come. Heaven is the real prize and we must avoid all things that could jeopardize this precious gift from our Lord. I often think of Grandpa when he talked about the mother lode just waiting to be discovered at his goldmine. He would get so excited just thinking about it. Now that Grandpa is in Heaven, I'm sure he gives little thought to his once earthly treasure.

There is nothing wrong with wanting to travel around the world or finding our mother lode as long as we do not compromise our relationship with God by doing so. On the other hand, there is nothing wrong with living your entire life without traveling more than a hundred-mile radius. The things we don't get to experience in this life will more than be made up for in Heaven. Our faith in God is the mother lode and spending eternity with Him is our hope.

Everything we do matters and every second counts; therefore, we need to take full advantage of this allotted time while we still can. As Christians, we have a lot to look forward to and just the thought of spending eternity with God should be enough to get us through whatever situation we face. Again, it all comes down to faith which can only come from our Heavenly Father. Replacing our fear with faith allows us to surrender our lives to God. When we truly trust in our Lord, we can be confident that He will always be there for us no matter how good or bad our situation may become. We will never be alone in our struggles or our accomplishments because we share all things with Christ. We must remember that God is far superior to us and the only way to bridge this gap is through faith.

This is why it can be hard for us to truly have faith in God because we try and do it through our own intellect which will always fall short.

Our inability to understand God has even led some people of faith to unbelief. To avoid this, we have to humble ourselves and come to the realization that there is something greater than ourselves. Faith demands that we come out of our comfort zone and reach out into the unknown where we feel the most vulnerable to failure. As Christians, we accept this vulnerable state because we trust that God will take care of us. Heaven will more than make up for our suffering in this life and we can thank our mighty Creator for such a wonderful gift. We should be obedient, not only because we want to go to Heaven, but more importantly, we do this out of love for God and want to please Him in this life and throughout eternity.

My great grandpa (third from the left) with three companions at a camp on their way up to the Neglected Mine, early 1900s.

Great Grandpa's Neglected Mine with crew that became famous in the Southwest Mountains of Colorado, early 1900s.

My mom and her brothers (front) along with two friends (back) on a float for the Fiesta Parade promoting Grandpa and his brother's Packard Jeep dealership. 1950

Grandpa by his 206 Cessna airplane, around 1980.

Grandpa coming out of his goldmine in his 80's.

Mom and Dad's wedding picture. My mom's parents and grandma (left), my dad's parents (right). 1962

My son playing first base in a regular season game. In a separate summer league, our team made it to the state playoff tournament, 2009. After a good effort, we ended up losing 13 to 7 to the team that won the state championship. Out of eight teams we tied for 4th.

Son smashing a ball for a double at the state championship game referenced on the previous page. Copyright © Catchlight Photography. All Rights Reserved. Used by permission.

Chapter 6

Death

John 11:25-26

> *Jesus said to her, "I am the resurrection and the life.*
> *He who believes in me will live, even though he dies;*
> *and whoever lives and believes in me will never die.*
> *Do you believe this?"*

Death is probably the most difficult challenge we face as Christians. The loss of a loved one or something that threatens our own life can push our faith to the limit, and if we're not careful, we can find ourselves blaming God. This only makes the healing process more difficult because without God in our lives, frustration, doubt, and fear leave us with no sense of purpose or direction. Fortunately for us, our loving Creator never abandons us no matter how bad we treat Him. His unconditional love remains true regardless of the situation or circumstance.

Jesus knows our pain because he experienced a horrible death in the mental, spiritual, and physical sense. Jesus also suffered death's sting through the loss of family and friends. The loss of His father, Joseph, was probably His most difficult experience with death. The news of John the Baptist's death greatly disturbed Him especially when He was told that John had been beheaded. From Scripture we also know that Jesus was deeply disturbed and even wept when Mary cried out to Him and expressed her pain from the loss of her brother Lazarus. (John 11:32-35)

> When Mary reached the place where Jesus was and saw him, she fell at his feet and said, "Lord, if you had been here, my brother would not have died." When Jesus saw her weeping, and the Jews who had come along with her also weeping, he was deeply moved in spirit and troubled. "Where have you laid him?" he asked. "Come and see, Lord," they replied. Jesus wept.

I feel that Jesus' sorrow went beyond His friend's temporary death – He was showing us how much He hated it in general and the sadness it brings to humankind. Jesus knew His purpose in this world was to conquer death through His crucifixion, resurrection, and ascension. (John 11:38-43)

> Jesus, once more deeply moved, came to the tomb. It was a cave with a stone laid across the entrance. "Take away the stone," he said. "But, Lord," said Martha, the sister of the dead man, "by this time there is a bad odor, for he has been there four days."
>
> Then Jesus said, "Did I not tell you that if you believed, you would see the glory of God?"
>
> So they took away the stone. Then Jesus looked up and said, "Father, I thank you that you have heard me. I knew that you always hear me, but I said this for the benefit of the people standing here, that they may believe that you sent me."
>
> When he had said this, Jesus called in a loud voice, "Lazarus, come out!" The dead man came out, his

hands and feet wrapped with strips of linen, and a cloth around his face. Jesus said to them, "Take off the grave clothes and let him go."

All in Heaven must have been rejoicing for this was a prelude of Christ's own death and resurrection that would finally put an end to death's sting giving all people the hope of eternal life.

Watching His dear friends, and especially His beloved mother Mary suffer terribly as they watched His crucifixion play out to the end, had to be one of the most difficult challenges of His life on Earth. Even in His worst moments of suffering, Jesus cared for and honored His mother, the most blessed woman who ever lived. (John 19:26-27)

> *When Jesus saw his mother there, and the disciple whom he loved standing nearby, he said to his mother, "Dear woman, here is your son," and to the disciple, "Here is your mother." From that time on, this disciple took her into his home.*

Jesus never gave up on anyone and continued to take care of His children, even to the point of assuring a common criminal that he would be with Him in paradise because of his repentant heart and faith in Christ. (Luke 23:40-43)

> *. . . But the other criminal rebuked him. "Don't you fear God," he said, "since you are under the same sentence? We are punished justly, for we are getting what our deeds deserve. But this man has done nothing wrong."*
>
> *Then he said, "Jesus, remember me when you come into your kingdom."*
>
> *Jesus answered him, "I tell you the truth, today you will be with me in paradise."*

The thief on the cross gives all of us hope, no matter how bad we think we have been in this life. Jesus wants all of us to go to Heaven and will do everything in His mighty, loving power to help each one of us achieve eternal life.

† † †

Eternity is a difficult concept to comprehend as is the Trinity, the creation of the universe, and all the other great mysteries of God that go well beyond our limited knowledge. It is understandable but a big mistake when we try to limit God to our own understanding. The God we have in our minds is usually too small and if we can't figure it out on our own, we sometimes think God can't either.

As Christians, we have to quit falling into the trap of thinking for God; instead, we should put our trust in Him and let God be God. In order to "let go and let God," we need to look back on all His accomplishments in our lives and should constantly remind ourselves who we are dealing with and how magnificent He really is! Only through faith can we know Him and accept His ways even if we do not understand them. We have to humble ourselves by never thinking we have everything under control. Only God is omnipotent; therefore, we must completely rely on Him for all our needs. The following well-known Scripture sums this up beautifully. (Proverbs 3:5-8)

> *Trust in the LORD with all your heart and lean not on your own understanding; in all your ways acknowledge him, and he will make your paths straight. Do not be wise in your own eyes; fear the LORD and shun evil. This will bring health to your body and nourishment to your bones.*

Personal Loss of a Loved One

I never gave death much thought until it hit home a little over 13 years ago. It was late January 1996 when I received a call from my mom. Her voice is usually upbeat, but on this occasion, it was deeply distraught and I knew something was wrong. Without hesitation, she gave me the horrible news that ultimately changed my family's life. My dad was diagnosed with late-term lung cancer but further tests would have to be conducted to confirm the initial results. After hearing this, an intense weakness spread throughout my body and I was overcome with a type of fear that I hope to never experience again.

I informed my wife of the crisis and explained that we would have to leave right away. In a rush, we left late the following evening without checking the weather forecast. About half way through our trip deep in the rugged Rocky Mountains, we ran into severe winter weather in a wide flat region known for its dangerous driving conditions. Snow blows off miles of flat fields onto and across the road from both directions. A blizzard had come out of the north which quickly became a whiteout. A State Patrol officer set up a temporary roadblock diverting traffic over a steep mountain pass. At least there the snow drifting across the road wouldn't be as bad. Now all we had to worry about was sliding off one of the sharp hairpin turns that worked its way up to the summit of a mountain and then back down again.

Despite the potential dangers ahead, I was determined to reach our destination so we decided to forge ahead. All I could focus on was the crisis that awaited me at the end of our journey. Thank God we were able to literally plow through the snow without incident and we safely made it to my parents' house.

As we sat parked in their driveway, part of me wanted to turn around and go back and pretend this nightmare wasn't really happening. I knew seeing my dad eye to eye would be extremely difficult considering the fact that our relationship was never expressed on an emotional basis. We had never hugged or exchanged "I love you's," but instead it was a working relationship.

† † †

My brother and I from an early age had worked for my dad in his construction business and our personal conversations were usually limited to what was accomplished at the end of the day's work. If we weren't working together we were usually off hunting or fishing. It was times while out in nature that we had our best conversations. Don't get me wrong; as I explained earlier, my dad was an honest, hard-working, intelligent man, but like the rest of us, he wasn't perfect. Though Dad by the grace of God, was able to quit drinking ten years before his diagnosis of lung cancer, he could not stop smoking no matter how hard he tried. Our family knew his habit would eventually make him sick but when it finally happened, we were still taken by surprise.

I never really understood what kind of relationship Dad had with God. He didn't go to church with our family and he rarely talked about Christ with us. We often talked openly about our Lord when Dad was in our presence, but he usually sat there silent, not engaged in our conversations. I often wondered what he was thinking about when we shared our Christian experiences. He was an analytical type of thinker and was a genius in mathematics. As with many other brilliant minds, faith in something you can't prove on paper can be difficult to accept.

† † †

After much thought, we got out of the car and my mom immediately greeted us with concerned, tear-filled eyes as we exchanged hugs. We found out that my dad was staying at the hospital overnight as they had conducted another series of tests. I was actually relieved that he wasn't there which gave me more time to mentally prepare myself for the inevitable. It was late so we all went directly to bed. Surprisingly, I quickly fell asleep but awoke in the middle of the night and had forgotten about Dad's condition. After lying there for a moment, my memory came back and the reality of the situation set in hard, which left me tossing and turning the rest of the night.

Early the next morning, exhausted, we headed to the hospital to see my dad. When we arrived, my hands were drenched with sweat and I wondered if I could even go through with it. Never before had I been placed in such an awkward situation. I told my wife and mom that I wanted to meet with him alone and they understood.

While walking down the hallway which led to his room, I saw a man in a green hospital gown sitting in a wheelchair, staring out the window. I've rarely seen my dad in anything other than his normal clothes and never in a wheelchair, so at first glance I didn't recognize him. It was a shocking sight to see him sitting there looking so helpless. My brother and sister arrived at that moment which made me feel better having someone else with me when facing Dad. As we all walked closer, he broke out of his gaze and saw us coming. I could tell that he was embarrassed to be seen that way. He had hardly been sick a day in his life and had just recently climbed a steep mountain while elk hunting. Yet there he was, humiliated by his condition, but he knew he had no choice but to face his dilemma.

The closer we got to Dad, the faster my heart pounded and I realized it was going to be harder to face him than I had anticipated. I clearly remember my first words, "Hey Dad, is this really happening?" He just slowly shook his head and nodded in acknowledgement. For the first time, we saw tears well up in his eyes which sent a series of painful emotions running through my heart. Dad explained that the test results confirmed that he indeed had late stage lung cancer and was only given several months to live. It was unfortunate that he had to get this horrible news on his birthday. We all told him not to give up, that we would be praying for him, and would do everything we could to help out. I told Dad that I would stay as long as necessary to help them get through this crisis. This was tough stuff, something unlike I'd ever experienced before and hoped would never happen again.

In the following days the usual procedures were administered, radiation, chemotherapy, and laser treatments to help reduce the size of the tumor to enable my dad to breath better. We were all praying for a healing and we shared this with him. The first month would see my dad in and out of the hospital which gave him little time to work so I had to take over all the jobs he presently had going and began soliciting new contracts to help them out financially. My mom, who is a licensed dietician, had to continue working to help pay for the bills that kept pouring in from all the medical costs. On top of it all, my parents were in the last stages of building a new home and had a lot of work left to finish.

Despite our efforts, Mom and Dad were still short on money so we decided to rent out a large shop building located on their property. We told Dad our plans and he agreed it would be for the best. To our amazement, we were able to rent the building out to a company who operated their business just a few miles down the road. All they needed it for was storage and agreed to let us use one-quarter of it for our own needs. The rent was almost exactly what Mom needed to cover the house payment. Little did we know that Dad had asked God to help us rent it out and God's quick answer to my dad's prayer helped build his new found faith. These were trying times but our family pulled together and through Christ's grace, we were able to keep our heads above water and continue forward.

Through the month of February, the cancer in his lungs became more aggressive and grew rapidly. His doctor claimed it was the fastest growing cancer he had ever seen. That wasn't good news and from that point forward, they increased the laser treatment used to help burn away the tumor to free his air passages. The cancer was growing so fast that it was literally plugging up his lungs. After the treatment he would feel better, but within a few days the cancer would grow back and new treatment would be required. As things got worse, we intensified our prayers and openly laid our hands on Dad and asked God to heal him.

March came and his condition had turned for the worse, to the point that the doctor told us that he only had a few days to live. The doctor felt he had no choice but to be more aggressive with the laser treatment and warned us that Dad probably wouldn't make it through the procedure. Regardless, Dad decided to go ahead with it. Just in case, we all came to the hospital to give our last good-byes. I got the strangest feeling thinking it could be the last time on Earth I would see him. Although it was difficult, I told Dad for the first time that I loved him.

I'll never forget the way my brother reacted as the nurse began wheeling Dad off towards surgery. He just waved his hand and said, "Good-bye." Dad responded with a brief hand wave and replied, "I'll be working hard building a house for all of you in Heaven." We never expected a comment like that and wondered if he was trying to tell us that our prayers were not in vain and that God had touched him in a miraculous way? Regardless, it gave us hope that he had come to know our Lord.

It turned out that he survived the laser surgery and God had given all of us a second chance. He felt much better but was still too weak to come home. After a few weeks went by he once again took a turn for the worse so we all went to his bed side and gathered for prayer. Something happened that night that only God could be responsible for. As we were about to pray, Dad reached out his hand to take mine. This made me feel extremely uncomfortable. First of all, this was the first time he had offered to openly pray with us and second, we had never held hands before. Uncomfortable or not, I grasped his hand and we all prayed the Our Father. To say the least, it was a very special moment. God's presence was with us that night and Dad received a miraculous healing, physical and spiritual.

Several days later the doctor was amazed at how much better he was feeling and even suggested that we take him home for a few days. We all thought his physical healing would be permanent. I picked

Dad up from the hospital late in the afternoon and remember how anxious he was to finally come home again.

As we were pulling down the long narrow driveway leading to his home, I couldn't help but notice what a beautiful evening was unfolding before us. The sun was just starting to set behind the majestic Rocky Mountains and the sky was lit up with a dazzling fiery red that appeared almost angelic. To me, it was as if God was doing it just for my dad and this special gift didn't go unnoticed. Dad proclaimed, "What a beautiful sunset God has given us! After spending so much time in the hospital I now realize how much I've taken all of this for granted." What he said may not sound profound to someone who didn't know him, but to me, it was as if the gates of Heaven had opened up and portrayed all its glory! Our whole family had prayed for years for Dad to accept Christ and I had my doubts that it would ever happen. But there on that special evening, he was letting me know that he had come to believe in our Lord.

We had a joyful family dinner. Later that evening after everyone had gone to sleep, I lay awake staring out the window deep into a starlit night. Intently praying, God inspired me with the following words, "I am more concerned with the soul than the body."

A few days later, Dad suddenly became worse again and we had to take him back to the hospital. It seemed like it all happened so fast. They ran some tests and found out the cancer had spread to his liver which all but guaranteed the outcome. He had a severe reaction to the contrast die used to conduct the test and his scarred lung tissue caused from all the laser treatments started to hemorrhage. His lungs soon filled with fluid and my mom stood by his side all night and prayed with him. She encouraged him to say Jesus as he breathed in and out and this brought him some needed comfort. Dad slowly passed away in the loving arms of my mom and early the next morning on a cold snowy day, I received word that he had died.

† † †

I'll never forget going to his hospital room and seeing Dad in a reclined position with his lifeless, pale body just lying there motionless in his bed. This was my first close-up experience with death and it changed my life forever. The reality of death was now real and I quickly became aware of how fragile life could be. The need to always be ready to meet Jesus took on a whole new meaning – there is nothing more important than spending eternity with Christ. There is no source of human pleasure that can compare with this wonderful gift that awaits all that are written in the book of life.

We cannot be like my dad who took the chance of missing out on Heaven most of his life. He was very fortunate to have had the necessary time to accept Jesus. Dad faced several near death experiences that could have jeopardized his relationship with Christ but God in His mercy repeatedly saved him.

Second Chances

When only a young boy, a gang of hoodlums grabbed Dad while he was walking over a bridge and they threw him over the side into the icy cold river below that was swollen from spring run off. It was worse than it sounds because he had not yet learned to swim.

What a terrifying swimming lesson it must have been. Somehow, he managed to dog paddle to shore and was probably the reason why I never saw him get into the water above his head.

On another occasion in his teenage years, Dad, with several friends aboard, was driving too fast around a sharp corner in his 57 Chevy. The car slid off the road and went airborne off the side of a steep hillside landing upside down in a small river. Miraculously, they all survived with only minor injuries.

Bar Fight

When I was in grade school, my mom and dad went to a bar with some friends in a small mountain town some 20 miles from home. Dad had too much to drink and got into a scuffle with some hardcore locals who didn't appreciate outsiders. Mom was able to calm Dad down and they spent the rest of the evening without incident.

On their way out while going back to their car, Mom noticed that the men who confronted them in the bar were waiting outside for them. She pretended she didn't notice them and grabbed Dad's hand and hurried towards their car. One of the men started to follow them and now Dad noticed who it was so he turned to confront him. Their friends had already left so my parents were on their own. The Moon was full that night and Mom noticed the man had a large shiny object behind his back who was now standing directly in front of Dad. They started arguing with each other and Mom suddenly realized the man was holding a large knife. Without even thinking, she kicked the man directly in the privates momentarily incapacitating him. She then used her elbow to hit Dad in the stomach which knocked the wind out of him. She grabbed Dad who was now standing hunched over and literally threw him into their car. By this time, the man had recovered enough to go after her and she barely escaped to the safety of her car. In a rage, the man reached his hand into her partially opened window and tried to grab her. Mom quickly rolled the window up trapping his hand. She started up the engine and put the pedal to the metal. The man was forced to run along side the car until he was finally able to free himself. Mom looked back and saw him jumping up and down cursing at her. By this time, Dad had recovered and yelled, "Were you trying to get me killed?" He didn't know the man had a knife behind his back and Dad in his intoxicated condition wouldn't have stood a chance.

God had given Mom supernatural strength. She had never done anything like that before and was convinced that a miracle took place that night which ultimately prevented Dad from severe injury or even death.

Fishing Adventure

Later in his life when I was a teenager, Dad and a friend decided to go fishing at the bottom of a steep, rugged, mountain gorge where a small but turbulent river lay. After a hard forty-five minute hike downhill, they reached the stream by mid afternoon. The fishing was spectacular and was well worth their efforts. Dad fished down stream and his partner fished up. He became so consumed with the great fishing that Dad failed to notice a storm that was quickly approaching from the west. Down in the canyon it was hard to see what was going on with the weather and before he knew it, the sky quickly closed up and within minutes it began to rain. The rain wasn't the main problem – it was the intense gusts of wind. Dad claimed it was blowing so hard that he could hardly stand up.

Instead of trying to race back up the steep canyon to his truck, he decided to search for a place to weather out the storm. He hadn't even made it back to the trail head before darkness set in with no sign of his friend. Dad said he had never experienced such darkness and literally could not see his hand placed in front of his eyes. He managed to light a cigarette which gave him some relief but the conditions worsened. Dad knew he had to find some type of shelter soon. His clothes were drenched and he began to shiver from the cold and windy, rain-soaked night.

Crawling on his hands and knees, he finally managed to find a rock ledge protruding out enough to provide some overhead cover. He gathered up some pine needles and made a much needed fire. It felt good to feel the warmth of the flames against his cold body.

After sitting there for awhile, the bottom of his legs started to feel hot, causing him to jump up. Dad realized that his fire had gotten out of control and was spreading out into the forest. Frantically, he took off his coat and used it in a desperate attempt to extinguish the wind-whipped flames. From his efforts and mostly from the rain, the fire was finally put out. Dad decided not to start another fire especially since the rain had just stopped and the winds had intensified. Instead, he hunkered down under the ledge and pulled pine needles around him to help stay warm.

While all this was going on, I was attending an overnight youth lock-in at the local YMCA. I remember getting a call from my mom around 10:00 p.m. informing me that Dad had not made it back to his truck that evening. His friend decided to hike out despite the dangerous conditions and was fortunate to make it safely back to his truck where he waited several hours for Dad's return. He told my mom not to worry because we all knew how experienced Dad was out in the woods. That thought helped a little but the intensity of the storm caused us great concern. His friend told Mom that he would organize a search party if Dad wasn't out of the canyon by daybreak.

The wind was blowing so hard at the YMCA, at times it felt as if the roof would blow off. We found out the next day that wind gusts had exceeded 100 miles per hour. Meanwhile, Dad was still out there, hunkered down in the darkness with the coming of dawn as his only hope. He claimed the night went on for an eternity and hardly slept a wink. When it finally became light enough for him to make out his surroundings, his heart nearly jumped out of his chest. He was perched on the edge of a tall cliff and quickly realized that if he had ventured only a few feet further, he would have surely fallen to his death. Our prayers were answered and he returned home later that morning. Through God's wonderful grace, He protected my dad and gave him an extension on life.

Gracious God

There were other times when his life could have ended but God kept saving him because He knew Dad would eventually come to know

Him. God wants all of us to be with Him more than anything else and will do everything possible to get us to Heaven.

Yes, God used cancer as a means to save my dad and no, God didn't cause his cancer. Instead, Dad brought it upon himself by his years of smoking but God who is perfect found a way to turn a family tragedy into something beautiful. Although God may not have answered our prayers for Dad's complete physical recovery, we thanked Him for answering our prayers for his conversion. I look forward to the day when I will be reunited with him and see him standing perfect in Christ's love – that will be a wonderful day indeed!

Close Call

A short time after Dad's death, I was working on a job with one of his former employees and longtime friend. Later that day, we ran out of materials so I sent him over to the construction yard located at my mom's property only a few miles from our jobsite. While running a backhoe, I noticed he was traveling extremely fast as he was returning to the jobsite. When he pulled up and got out of his truck, there was a look of horror in his eyes. He quickly informed me that my wife and son had been in a terrible car accident. In a shaky voice he went on to tell me that their car was mangled and everyone had already been removed from the scene. I instantly went into a state of shock. First my dad had died and now I didn't know the fate of my own family.

Terrified, I jumped into my truck and quickly headed down the road towards the nightmare that was quickly being revealed. On the way to the accident scene I started to pray out loud, harder than I ever had before. When I arrived and saw the extent of the damage, I thought for sure my wife and son had been killed. The back end of their car was completely smashed in and broken glass was everywhere. The horrible reality of the situation began to set in and I frantically tried to get the number of the local hospital but my cell phone wouldn't roam in that area.

I started driving towards the nearest town and along the way, I was finally able to reach an operator who transferred my call to the hospital. When the receptionist answered the phone, I gave her my wife's name and she immediately asked if I was referring to a young lady and her child. "Yes!" I exclaimed. By that time I was swerving all over the road about to get into an accident of my own. The receptionist located my wife and put her on the phone. As soon as I heard her voice, a huge weight was lifted off my soul. "Are you alright?" I nervously asked while still swerving on the road. I must have sounded like a mad man because she told me to calm down and informed me that our son had suffered a concussion but was conscious and appeared to be doing ok.

I asked myself how this could be possible since the back of their car was smashed almost beyond recognition and they were not only alive, but appeared to be free from major injury. I told my wife it was a miracle that they were ok and would be at the hospital soon. When I got off the phone, my tears of fear were replaced with streaming tears of joy which made it difficult to see the road ahead. This terrifying event had unleashed all the emotions pent up from my dad's recent death compounded by the thought of almost losing my wife and son – it was more than I could bear.

After finally arriving at the hospital, I ran into the emergency room. Upon entering, I saw my wife standing at my son's bedside, stroking his little head. Actually seeing them in person was proof that they were really alright. We exchanged hugs and I bent over and gave our son a gentle kiss on his forehead. At first he seemed ok, but moments later he started vomiting which scared the daylights out of both of us. We instantly called the nurse who calmed us down by assuring us that this type of reaction was normal after suffering a concussion. To be on the safe side, she informed us that they would perform a CT scan to make sure his brain wasn't damaged. The scan was a scary experience for the little guy but proved to be well worth the effort. After reviewing the scan, the doctor gave us the good news that everything looked normal and after some much needed rest, our son would be fine.

Again, we both openly praised Jesus for miraculously protecting our family. My wife suffered some injuries but after being rehabilitated, she has been able to lead a normal life. We all realize that it could have been much worse.

† † †

After visiting the damaged car at a local wrecking yard, a close-up inspection confirmed that God had indeed performed a miracle. The impact from the other car had cracked the back of our son's car seat in half. If the impact had penetrated any further, our son would not be alive today. God through his great mercy and love, held the other car back just enough to allow our son to live.

The driver responsible for this accident was a young teenage girl who had several friends with her. My wife was stopped at a busy two-lane highway to turn left into my mom's driveway. There were several oncoming cars so she had to wait before turning. As she looked into her review mirror, she could see a car coming off in the distance. As the car got closer, it appeared it wasn't slowing down. She then looked forward to see if it was ok to turn, and without warning, the car behind her slammed into the back of her car while traveling over 50 miles per hour. The impact was tremendous and it sent her car spinning into the oncoming traffic lane. The automobile that hit her was much larger which added to the force of the collision. None of the passengers from the other vehicle were hurt but the driver came out screaming hysterically, apologizing for the accident. She was too busy talking with her friends and failed to notice my wife's car stopped in front of her. It was only at the last second that she turned right to try and avoid the collision. This last second reaction helped reduce the impact by channeling more of the energy to the right side of the car which in turn helped to save my son's life. Because of this, there was more damage to the right back side of the car than to the left. My son was in the backseat on the left side. That morning before the accident, my wife changed his car seat from the right to the left side and didn't know why. I don't think this was a coincidence; rather, the mighty power of God was at work.

Airplane Adventures

When I was in seventh grade, Grandpa and Grandma took my brother, sister, and me with them on a trip to Long Beach, California, in their six-seat, 206 Cessna airplane. During our journey, we made a pit stop at a small airport located on the rim of the Grand Canyon. As the control tower gave us permission to land on our final descent, I noticed a plane coming directly toward us and yelled at Grandpa to alert him of the impending danger. He saw the plane and quickly veered to the right and successfully avoided a collision.

I'll never forget Grandpa yelling at the control tower operator who had mistakenly brought two planes in to land at the same time. It all happened so fast that he hardly had time to react. The man in the control tower apologized but Grandpa couldn't shake off the incident which caused him to bring us in for a hard landing. After stretching our legs and refueling the plane, we became airborne again and had the privilege of flying down the center of the Grand Canyon which was an incredible sight to see.

Later in the flight while over Palm Springs, a small plane traveling the opposite direction suddenly appeared out of nowhere and missed colliding with us by only a few hundred feet. Air traffic is required by law to maintain an even or odd elevation depending on which direction they are traveling. The plane was not following this rule which nearly caused an accident. Grandpa shook it off and we continued on our eventful journey.

As we approached Los Angeles, we encountered a massive layer of smog that greatly reduced our visibility. I remember my brother and I helped Grandpa by getting the aviation maps out to help locate our destination at Long Beach International Airport. After we found it, we had to circle around for awhile before we landed due to the heavy air traffic. Grandpa finally received permission to land. To our surprise, as soon as the wheels touched the ground, the plane started shaking violently. Without hesitation, Grandpa quickly aborted the landing and became airborne again. He told us to look out the window to see if anything was wrong and we immediately noticed the right rear tire was completely flat and panic started to set in. My brother wasn't fazed but my sister started crying and Grandma started praying out loud as she always does in times of trouble. Before it got out of control, Grandpa told us to stay calm and reassured us that he would get us down safely. He then contacted the control tower and told them our situation. They immediately shut down an entire runway and moved emergency gear into that location. After they were ready, they instructed Grandpa to come in for another landing. I have never been so afraid while approaching the runway not knowing if we would make it.

As the plane touched down, the incredible shaking returned and we started to veer off the edge of the runway. He throttled the plane once again for another touch-and-go and we became airborne again. On the third attempt, Grandpa realized that he would have to slow the plane down as much as possible before landing. This posed a problem because at a slower speed, we probably wouldn't be able to take off again if the landing wasn't successful. He radioed the control tower informing them of his plan and they had no choice but to allow him to try it. Grandpa was honest and told us that our landing would be extremely rough. He asked us to put our heads on our laps and say a prayer. I didn't know what to expect and feared for our lives. The plane once again started shaking violently as it touched the ground but because of the slower speed, he was able to control the plane and brought us to a safe stop. It felt so good to finally be down and I remember giving thanks to Grandpa and Jesus for saving us.

Grandpa never lost his cool and did a wonderful job keeping us safe. He was congratulated by the emergency team and they escorted us off the plane to the safety of the tarmac. Of course, Grandpa gave all the credit to God. It was determined that the tire was probably damaged by the hard landing earlier that day at the Grand Canyon Airport.

† † †

This wasn't the first time that Grandpa had an emergency landing. It happened several years earlier when he was solo test flying his plane after a mechanic had performed a routine tune-up on his engine. While flying around 10,000 feet above a small city, he suddenly lost all engine power and couldn't restart it. Grandpa called out, "Mayday-mayday-mayday!" on his radio. He gave the tower his exact location and then started looking for a spot to bring it down as he was quickly losing altitude.

Below him, he saw a football field located next to a school but there were kids playing on it so he searched for another site. Time was running out so he decided to land on an upward sloping hillside that appeared to be fairly free from obstacles. Grandpa hoped that the upward slope would help slow his momentum allowing the plane to stop faster. All was well when he first made contact with the ground; however, just before the plane came to a stop his left wing hit a small pinion tree causing his plane to flip upside down. The rescue workers arrived almost immediately and they went to work pulling Grandpa out of the wreckage. He was very fortunate to have only suffered a mild contusion to his forehead but he was extremely angry that his plane was damaged, especially since he had almost come out of it without incident.

Grandpa could have put others at risk by choosing a safer landing site on the football field, but instead he put the safety of the school children above his own. After an investigation, it was determined that a faulty fuel filter was to blame for the engine failure.

Update – September 14, 2009

After my wife's dad had suffered a small stroke, she was given the bad news that he was diagnosed with three aortic aneurysms that would require surgery to repair these life-threatening bulges in his arteries. Her dad was scheduled for surgery but he started having complications from the blood pressure medication he was on. Then a blood clot which had formed at one of his aneurysms started sending small particulates of debris into his arteries which became lodged in some smaller arteries/veins in his feet. The partial blockage caused a great deal of pain to his toes. One night it got so bad that he had to go to the emergency room.

Because of his deteriorating condition, my wife's youngest sister called and left a message asking if my wife would come before her dad's scheduled surgery. I listened to the message before my wife was home and was very moved by her sister's tearful plea for her to come. I immediately called the airline to see what was available.

About the same time, my wife arrived and I told her the news. She was shook up after hearing her sister's message. We both started searching for a flight and she found one online that would allow her to leave in three days. Just before she clicked the button to pay for the flight, the power went off for just a split second causing the computer screen to go blank. Frustrated, she rebooted her computer only to find the flight had doubled in price because it was now the last seat available. Meanwhile, I was on the phone with another company that agreed to give her an emergency medical discount which brought the price a little lower than her original online quote. This flight also allowed her to leave in two days giving her more time with her dad and family. It is amazing how God takes care of the details and this was only the beginning.

† † †

When she arrived, her dad was doing better and just being there in person brought her great relief. It started off as a wonderful time catching up with family, especially with her dad. But then unexpectedly something happened that changed everything.

My wife was planning on taking her dad to the doctor's office a few days after arriving. The morning of his appointment, my mother-in-law came into my wife's room asking for help to get my father-in-law out of bed. He was complaining that his back was really sore and was having a hard time getting up. They were concerned that it was related to his kidneys which had recently become compromised from the blood pressure medication and possibly from small blood clots that were partially blocking the arteries leading to his kidneys. They asked him where it hurt and he claimed it was high on his back just below his left arm pit. He said it felt like a pulled muscle. Since it wasn't in the kidney area, they dismissed it and told him to get some rest before his doctor's visit. The fact that he had gone to work the previous day and seemed fine also led them to believe it wasn't serious. Her mom then left to a bible study and my wife stayed behind to make sure he would be alright.

A few hours later, he got himself out of bed, got dressed, and came down stairs. By this time her mom had returned. He told them he didn't feel like going to the doctor's appointment. As he was saying this, they noticed his right arm was shaking and he looked extremely weak. His wife immediately called 911 and an ambulance arrived shortly. The paramedics found his blood pressure was dangerously low and his blood oxygen level nearly nonexistent. They rushed him to the hospital.

While my wife and her mom were following the ambulance, she called her sister to let her know what was happening and then she called me. After hearing what had happened, we were all thinking that his aneurysm had probably ruptured. For obvious reasons his life was in serious jeopardy. While at the local hospital, his condition had stabilized and they were able to determine that indeed the aneurysm had at least partially ruptured.

Thank God it happened while he was in bed where my wife and her mom could monitor his condition. If it had happened when he was alone, or worse yet while driving, it probably would have resulted in a tragic outcome. After conducting the necessary tests at the local hospital, he was then rushed to another hospital that specializes in this type of surgery. They prepared for emergency surgery and shortly afterward he was under the knife. This was a very complex procedure.

My wife and her family sent out prayer requests because they knew this would be a risky operation. They were told the chance of death resulting from this type of procedure is anywhere from 2-

15% pre-rupture depending on the health of the individual. The odds of death occurring after the aneurysm has ruptured can be over 50%. I personally knew two people that had a ruptured aneurysm who died within minutes after it happened. One man was shoveling snow off his roof and the other was eating dinner with family when it occurred. It was a quick gruesome death especially for family members who witnessed it. But there was my father-in- law, still alive, probably wondering what was next as the outcome of his own life was still in the balance.

It just so happened that the team of surgeons who have the best reputation for this type of procedure had just gotten back from vacation the day before and were available that evening to help save his life. The operation began early in the evening and went well into the early morning hours before it was complete (8 hours). The doctor came in the waiting room and informed my mother-in- law and wife that the surgery went as well as could be expected considering the circumstances. That was good news and helped to ease the tensions that were building throughout the long night.

God had spared his life because He still had other plans for him. Her dad had been struggling with his faith and now he was granted more time to reconcile with Christ and others around him. Not to mention the fact that he would be able to spend more time with his family and friends who dearly love him. God is good!

† † †

When they saw him in his room for the first time, it was a hard thing to witness. He had multiple IVs and wires hooked up to him with a breathing tube down his throat to allow the respirator to do its job. His face and extremities were swollen and the seriousness of his situation became more real. My mom works in a hospital and informed me that this type of surgery, especially if the patient has ruptured, can be a long up-and-down recovery that can last up to a month in the hospital depending on the patient.

By the second day, he was doing a little better but still had the breathing tube in. The fact that he had smoked most of his life wasn't helping anything. However, he had taken the doctor's advice to quit smoking at least two months prior to any surgery. His obedience, in part, most likely helped to save his life. My wife and her family stayed at his bed side to comfort and aid him in any way possible. A cardiac nurse informed them that she had been doing this for over 20 years and had never seen a patient do so well with this type of surgery. This was even better news! To keep them from getting too hopeful, she cautioned them that he had a long way to go before a full recovery could be expected. They were just thankful that he was alive. The timing of the whole event couldn't have been better for my wife. She never expected to be there for his surgery; rather, just to spend time with him while he was still relatively healthy. Instead, she was able to do both.

When it came time for her to come home, she had reservations about leaving her dad who was still not fully conscious three days after surgery. I was able to get the airlines to extend her flight one more day which gave her more time to spend with her dad and family. I reminded my wife that God was in control and had already saved her dad's life. I told her that no matter the outcome, they did all they could by lining up the best surgeons in the area, the best hospital available for this type of procedure, and a lot of people were praying for him. Her dad was blessed to have all of this line up so perfectly. It was now clear why my sister-in-law was inspired by the Holy Spirit to call my wife to come earlier than planned. God knows the future and already knew that this would happen. It is amazing to look back and see how He prepares us for our trials in life.

Coming Home

On my wife's return trip home it was a perfectly calm, starlit night. We live only minutes from a small regional airport so I decided to wait until she called before picking her up.

While I was getting ready to go to the airport, I thought I heard a low rumble noise that sounded far-off in the distance. Then I heard it again. This time, I went outside to see what it was and off in the distance, I could see a major lightning storm headed our way. I prayed that her flight would hurry up and get here before the storm arrived. They had a 15-minute delay trying to balance out their small jet's heavy load. Unfortunately, those 15 minutes put them in a direct collision course with one of the most dynamic thunderstorms I'd ever experienced. "If only they could land before it gets here," I kept nervously telling myself. Then right at 10:00 p.m. all heck broke loose.

At first, the wind picked up and then the storm quickly followed. Lightning was striking all around us and the wind was blowing out of control. I ran outside and raised my hands toward the angry sky and pleaded with God to divert the storm away from the airport. Almost immediately, as if God was responding, a huge bolt of lightning struck less than a mile away, exposing me with its brilliant light for the madman I had become. I saw my son looking out the window staring at me with concerned eyes. After the lightning strike, he yelled at me to come inside before I was struck by another blast from above. When I came inside he just stared at me for a moment and then told me I was crazy. I frantically replied by telling him that he had better pray like never before because Mom was up there being tossed around like a tumble weed. He just nervously laughed and told me to get a hold of myself.

The plane was now 30 minutes late with no call yet from my wife. I thought for sure the violent weather had ripped them out of the sky. I have been in small planes before in conditions much better and was still bounced around like a ping pong ball. My worse nightmare was starting to become a reality. About that time, the weather finally started to break a little so my son and I went outside to see if we could spot or hear her plane. Off in the distance, I spotted a small bright light low on the horizon. At first I thought it was a star peeking through a small break in the clouds. My son said it was definitely a plane. I answered, "But it's not moving." He replied, "It just looks like it's not because it's coming directly at us." The bright object started turning left towards the airport which confirmed that it was a plane. My son was right again. I immediately felt a great sense of relief but still wasn't a hundred percent sure it was her plane.

We both quickly got into the car and headed for the airport. While speeding down our driveway, my cell phone rang. I thanked Jesus and then answered it. Before she could say a word I told her, "You're never flying again!" She replied, "Well, I'm fine now." I took that to mean the flight was really rough. My fear turned into anger because I was mad that they would fly in such dangerous weather. After picking her up, she said the flight was actually really smooth because the pilot climbed above the clouds and informed the passengers that they would have to circle for 20 minutes until the storm passed through. She could see the lightning off in the distance and prayed that God would provide them an opening to safely land. God granted her request and it was so good to see her on the ground safe and sound.

I learned a valuable lesson from my son to trust God more and not panic. He kept a cool head and did a good job trying to calm me down. He reminded me how bad I did under pressure and I know he will never let me live it down especially since he secretly videotaped my hysteria. That's ok, I was very proud of him for keeping such a cool head when I flipped out.

Since my wife arrived home, her dad's condition has improved. It took nearly one-and-a-half weeks for him to be released from the intensive care unit and moved to the cardiac floor where patients have stabilized. This was good news and his condition continues to improve. He is now able to get out of his bed and walk around a bit. My wife's youngest sister recently sent her an email that made her appreciate how wonderful family is in troubled times. The email was as follows:

> When I saw Dad tonight, I told him how you were with Mom, at his bedside, every possible moment. We told him how impressed he would have been with you and your strength and compassion. He looked so touched and asked, "Really", and then he cried. Thought you would like to know . . .

A month later he was released from the hospital, is at home, and continues to make slow by steady progress.

† † †

Out of love, God saves all of us from death more than we know. When we meet Him in Heaven, the truths of our lives will be revealed and only then will we fully understand the purpose behind the events that shaped our destiny and of those around us. (Hebrews 2:14-15), (Revelation 21:4)

> *Since the children have flesh and blood, he too shared in their humanity so that by his death he might destroy him who holds the power of death—that is, the devil—and free those who all their lives were held in slavery by their fear of death.*

> *He will wipe every tear from their eyes. There will be no more death or mourning or crying or pain, for the old order of things has passed away."*

Chapter 7

Prayer

1 Thessalonians 5:16-18

> *Be joyful always; pray continually; give thanks in all circumstances, for this is God's will for you in Christ Jesus.*

The Apostle Paul tells us to pray continually and I have often wondered exactly what he meant and what responsibilities we have as Christians to follow this God-inspired teaching. Does this mean we have to literally say heartfelt prayers 24/7 or was Paul simply telling us to always keep God in our thoughts no matter what we're doing? Keeping God on our minds helps us to better foster a relationship with Him and it also prevents us from letting our guard down when we are tempted by sin. Just as a firewall is essential in protecting our computers, God is necessary to protect us from sin. It is a mistake to conveniently faze God in and out of our lives because without Him, we do not stand a chance against evil.

In the past while being tempted by sin, I have purposely tuned God out with the false belief that if I could distance myself from

Him, He wouldn't know what I was up to. What was I thinking? It is amazing how much our rationalizing minds can distort the reality of our particular situation. We can never hide anything from God and the following Scripture is a good reminder of this. (Psalm 139:1-4)

> *O LORD, you have searched me and you know me.*
>
> *You know when I sit and when I rise;*
>
> *you perceive my thoughts from afar.*
>
> *You discern my going out and my lying down;*
>
> *you are familiar with all my ways. Before a word is on my tongue*
>
> *you know it completely, O LORD.*

In the past I found having a picture of Jesus with me and looking at Him when contemplating a poor decision proved to be an effective tool. Having to look at our Lord directly in the eyes was extremely convicting.

A physical picture may not always be available so it is important that we create His image deep in our hearts and should always be looking and listening to Christ no matter what the situation. As soon as we take our minds off Him, we quickly become vulnerable to sin. (Ephesians 6:11,12, 16-18)

> *Finally, be strong in the Lord and in his mighty power. Put on the full armor of God so that you can take your stand against the devil's schemes. For our struggle is not against flesh and blood, but against the rulers, against the authorities, against the powers of this dark world and against the spiritual forces of evil in the heavenly realms.*

In addition to all this, take up the shield of faith, with which you can extinguish all the flaming arrows of the evil one. Take the helmet of salvation and the sword of the Spirit, which is the word of God. And pray in the Spirit on all occasions with all kinds of prayers and requests. With this in mind, be alert and always keep on praying for all the saints.

Without God's guiding light to show us the way, we instantly become blind with no sense of direction. Without Him it is like being in a room at night when the lights suddenly go out – complete and utter darkness. We need God in everything, big and small, and are helpless without Him. It is not up to us to decide what is right and wrong – the rules have already been carefully decided for us and if we want to be in our Lord's will, we must obey Him. In order to obey Him, we must always be aware of His presence in our lives. God did not make these rules to lord it over us, but rather to protect us.

Relationship

Without prayer, there can be no relationship with God. We all know that we only get as much out of something as we put into it. This is also true with our relationships with others whether it's with our spouse, a friend, a parent, our kids, a co-worker, our boss, or anyone else we're dealing with on a regular basis. Lack of communication can cause serious problems and if not dealt with appropriately, the relationship can fail. Communication is essential for the success of any relationship.

Some of us, including myself, make the mistake of thinking that just because God already knows everything, He doesn't need to hear how we feel. By doing this, we are missing the point in why we were created in the first place – so God can have fellowship with man and woman. He created us out of love and wants us to tell him everything down to the smallest detail. We could never talk too much to God unless of course it was out of disrespect. He desires that we think about Him every moment and wants us to be in constant communication with Him. God's relationship with us is not selfish; instead, His giving nature infinitely exceeds what He receives.

Just as married couples can experience an incredible feeling of passion, Christians can also experience this powerful force with our Creator when we are born again. This feeling may only last for a short period of time, but the outcome can last forever. It becomes part of the foundation in which we build our relationship with Christ. The hard part comes after the feelings calm down and we are left with the monotony of day-to-day living. At this point, it is even more necessary to stay close to God to get us through the dry periods.

Unfortunately for us, our physical body is very demanding and usually gets most of our attention while our soul can go hungry. If our soul becomes malnourished from a lack of spiritual food, our physical body will suffer as well no matter how full it becomes. Everything is interconnected. Our physical body is important and we have an obligation to take good care of it because it is the dwelling place of the Holy Spirit. However, we cannot let this overshadow our obligation to nourish our soul. As important as the physical body is, it cannot compare to the value of our soul.

If we are able, fasting from food can be an excellent way to place the soul ahead of the body. In the state of fasting, prayer can be especially powerful because the soul is not competing with the flesh. Some people cannot fast on food because of health reasons but can fast from other things that provide pleasure to their bodies. The most important thing is to take time out and remove the distractions that keep us from spending quality time with God.

Despite His busy schedule, Jesus always found time to have communion with His Father. He often climbed a mountain where He could have peace and quiet from all the distractions of the crowds that constantly followed Him. A mountain top may not be practical for all of us, but each person can find their own personal prayer closet where they can have uninterrupted quality prayer time with God. (Matthew 6:6)

> But when you pray, go into your room, close the door and pray to your Father, who is unseen. Then your Father, who sees what is done in secret, will reward you.

In between this quality time, we still need to continue praying to God. Just as we usually find the time to feed our bodies, there are plenty of opportunities throughout the day to pray. The "Our Father" is the most beautiful and perfect prayer because it was given to us by Jesus Himself. This prayer can be recited daily because it has all the ingredients necessary for us to live better Christian lives.

Whether it is heartfelt prayer, an act of charity, or just having God on our minds, it is all a form of prayer and is essential in maintaining a quality relationship with Christ. Consistent prayer is pleasing to God and it also enriches our own lives. Prayer is exercise for the soul. Without it, our soul becomes flabby, weak, malnourished, and anemic causing us to become more vulnerable to sin.

Trials

What about the times when it appears God is ignoring us, especially when there is a problem in our lives. It can be very difficult when we hear from a friend or watch on television where God touched other people in a miraculous way when our own prayer seems to go unanswered, almost as if God is purposely ignoring us. Paul experienced this same dilemma. (2 Corinthians 12:7-9)

> To keep me from becoming conceited because of these surpassingly great revelations, there was given

me a thorn in my flesh, a messenger of Satan, to torment me. Three times I pleaded with the Lord to take it away from me. But he said to me, "My grace is sufficient for you, for my power is made perfect in weakness."

Paul had repeatedly asked God to free him from an unknown problem, but according to Scripture, he was not delivered from his affliction. Instead, he just learned to accept it. Paul became a disciple of Christ and was able to heal others, but his own problem continued, causing him to suffer. I have often wondered what this affliction was. Instead of healing him, God chose to use Paul's suffering to help strengthen his faith just like He does with our own problems.

Sometimes I get so frustrated with God because I know that He can do anything and wonder why He lets my problems persist even when I plead with Him to end them. There have been times when this frustration has even led me into temporary unbelief. This behavior can be dangerous but is sometimes necessary for our faith. Like Paul, there have been many prophets of God that have experienced his type of suffering. It is all part of God's plan to test and strengthen our faith. This allows our relationship with Christ to become closer and more personal as we learn to trust Him to help us overcome our weaknesses.

It is ok to get angry with God as long as we don't forget who we are dealing with – we cannot cross over the line and lose respect and honor for God; however, we also need to feel free enough to lay it on the line. God can handle it and has heard everything we could possibly imagine. No sin is too great for Him to forgive and nothing takes Him by surprise or is beyond his control. Yes, God is never wrong but that does not mean we cannot openly express our feelings with Him. He created us to have relationship with Him which includes the good, the bad, and everything in between.

We all have something in our lives that we would like to change, especially when it causes us to suffer. It has been said that adversity builds character, but most of us feel we would be better off without it. Unfortunately, being tested is an integral part of being a Christian. God has told us through Scripture that we will be tested. (James 1:12)

> *Blessed is the man who perseveres under trial, because when he has stood the test, he will receive the crown of life that God has promised to those who love him.*

Being a Christian is not easy. That is why prayer and relationship with God is so important. We have to trust He will never abandon us no matter how small or large the problems we face. We also have to be careful not to become bitter or angry with God when things are not going our way. Our suffering can have great power if we offer it up to Jesus in the same way that He shed His precious blood at Calvary, to allow us to stand perfect in the presence of God. This came at a heavy price, but Jesus offered it up and willingly accepted His suffering because he loves us and wants us to be with Him now and in Heaven. (1 Peter 4:12-14,16)

> *Dear friends, do not be surprised at the painful trial you are suffering, as though something strange were happening to you. But rejoice that you participate in the sufferings of Christ, so that you may be overjoyed when his glory is revealed. If you are insulted because of the name of Christ, you are blessed, for the Spirit of glory and of God rests on you.*

Like Paul, we all have thorns in our lives and it is amazing how dialed into these problems we can become, even to the point of obsession. When this occurs, a slender person can look into a mirror and actually see themselves as overweight, or a depressed teen can talk themselves into ending their own life. That is why it is so important that we look for opportunities to encourage one another. As my pastor always says, "Let's remember to pray for one another – you never know what someone next to you might be going through."

It is equally important that we learn to focus not only on our own strengths, but on the strengths of others as well. One person may be good at math while another at music, someone may be an excellent athlete and yet another may be good at causing others to smile. We are all gifted by God and as Christians, we have a moral obligation to help ourselves and others discover these sometimes hidden talents. (Jeremiah 29:11)

> For I know the plans I have for you," declares the LORD, "plans to prosper you and not to harm you, plans to give you hope and a future.

Just as He did for Paul, God will help each one of us overcome our shortcomings and will make up for them in ways that we cannot even imagine. God created us and has given us everything we need to live successful Christian lives. We cannot measure our success through the world's standards; instead, we must use God's Holy Word as our guide. We cannot let the world get us down, even if it rejects us. Jesus tells us in the following scripture that we will be rejected just as He was rejected. (John 15:18-21)

> If the world hates you, keep in mind that it hated me first. If you belonged to the world, it would love you as its own. As it is, you do not belong to the world, but I have chosen you out of the world. That is why the world hates you. Remember the words I spoke to you: 'No servant is greater than his master'. If they persecuted me, they will persecute you also. If they obeyed my teaching, they will obey yours also. They will treat you this way because of my name, for they do not know the One who sent me.

That is why it is so important to develop relationships with other Christians who share the same goals and understand our way of life. We have to decide who we are going to follow, either the world or God – there is no in between, no compromise, and no middle ground. It is either God's way or no way. This is a lot easier to say in words, but in reality it is a difficult path to follow because the world will not accept us if we truly follow Him.

Does this mean that if we follow Jesus, everyone who is not a believer will hate us? I don't think that most unbelievers will hate us personally, but instead, some will hate our values because they are contrary to that of the world's. Does this mean we should only deal with other Christians? We are called to follow the example that Jesus gave us. He dealt with all types of people but there is one thing that is important to remember – Jesus never compromised His values nor can we when dealing with the world no matter what the consequence. This requires supernatural strength that can only come from God.

Consequences of Sin

In our culture sin is not only accepted, but is encouraged, even amongst some Christians. Let's face it, it is much easier to sin in our generation because we have modified God's word in order to fit in with society and have distorted His laws to help ease our consciences. The secular world has incredible influence over our decisions and if we are not careful, our faith can become watered down, causing us to forget who we are and what we believe in.

Some have commented that earlier generations were more obedient and did a better job following God's commandments. In my opinion, I don't think any generation was or is more righteous than any other; rather, we are all sinners, and have always been and will continue to be in desperate need of Christ's sanctifying grace. It is true that some past generations were held more accountable to sin. In the mid 1900's it was not acceptable for public radio and

TV networks to air explicit and graphic material. Today, however, movies that hardly raise an eyebrow would have caused a riot if shown only a few decades ago.

We have become more tolerant to sin. I'm not necessarily talking about mortal sins such a murder. Instead, I am emphasizing on subtle sins that can be damaging to our spiritual walk with Christ. James tells us that if we disobey one commandment we have violated them all. (James 2:8-12)

> For whoever keeps the whole law and yet stumbles at just one point is guilty of breaking all of it. For he who said, 'Do not commit adultery,' also said,
>
> 'Do not murder.' If you do not commit adultery but do commit murder, you have become a lawbreaker.

We need to entrench ourselves deep into God's holy presence. We are all vulnerable to sin and can only avoid it through a strong relationship with Christ. In other words, evil is all around us and without God, we do not stand a chance. (1 Peter 5:8-11)

> Be self-controlled and alert. Your enemy the devil prowls around like a roaring lion looking for someone to devour. Resist him, standing firm in the faith, because you know that your brothers throughout the world are undergoing the same kind of sufferings.
>
> And the God of all grace, who called you to his eternal glory in Christ, after you have suffered a little while, will himself restore you and make you strong, firm and steadfast. To him be the power forever and ever. Amen.

God doesn't force us to seek His protection. Rather, through His great love, He gave us a free will. We are blessed to have a Creator that allows us to make our own decisions; however, our actions have consequences in which we are directly responsible. Therefore, it is wrong to blame God for problems in our lives, especially when our decisions caused the problems. It becomes more difficult when tragedy strikes and we had nothing to do with it.

What about a young child who develops leukemia? What did they do to deserve such a cruel disease? In this case, it is easy to see why a parent would cry out to God in anger for their child's misfortune. God never intended for man or woman to become ill or that anyone should die. The following Scripture clearly addresses this. (Genesis 1:26,27)

> *Then God said, "Let us make man in our image, in our likeness, and let them rule over the fish of the sea and the birds of the air, over the livestock, over all the earth, and over all the creatures that move along the ground."*
>
> *So God created man in his own image, in the image of God he created him; male and female he created them.*

Because we chose to be disobedient, disorder entered the world and corrupted every living thing in it including people, nature, the elements, and even our DNA. The consequences from this tragic decision, to name a few, have resulted in murder, rape, torture, abuse, divorce, abortion, deceit, arrogance, false pride, chaotic weather patterns, abnormal genetic mutations, disease, and ultimately death. Instead of blaming God for our problems, we must first come to the realization that He is perfect; therefore, only good can come from Him.

If society continues to reject God and willingly chooses a life of sin, the moral, spiritual, and physical breakdown of our world will only get worse resulting in more people falling victim to this self-imposed suffering. God in His mercy gave us a free will and does not force us to follow Him. There are, however, consequences to sin and innocent people such as the young child with leukemia get caught in the crossfire.

On a lesser scale, no one in their right mind would jump out of an airplane without a parachute, yet many of us choose to go through life without Christ. Because we reject God, He may pull His guiding hand back a little to show us what happens when we are on our own. In this case, we are the ones causing our own judgment. When society becomes so hardened by their sins that they reach a point of no return, God has no choice but to judge them as He did in Noah's flood and later with Sodom and Gomorrah. Judgment was coming to Nineveh but the people repented, and out of His mercy, God spared them. (Jonah 3:1-5,10)

> *Then the word of the LORD came to Jonah a second time: "Go to the great city of Nineveh and proclaim to it the message I give you."*
>
> *Jonah obeyed the word of the LORD and went to Nineveh. Now Nineveh was a very important city—a visit required three days. On the first day, Jonah started into the city. He proclaimed: "Forty more days and Nineveh will be overturned." The Ninevites believed God. They declared a fast, and all of them, from the greatest to the least, put on sackcloth.*
>
> *When God saw what they did and how they turned from their evil ways, he had compassion and did not bring upon them the destruction he had threatened.*

Our fate depends on the choices we make. We have no one else to blame if we choose to rebel against our Lord. Only good can come from our Creator who is perfect in His righteousness. Fortunately for us, God is also the master at turning a bad situation into something positive.

So if God is perfect and our ways are evil, then why did Jesus ask us to be perfect? Is this an unrealistic expectation considering the fact that He knows how weak we are? God hates all sin and in His great wisdom and love for us, He offered up His only son, Jesus Christ, as a sacrifice for our sins, and by the shedding of Christ's precious blood, we are made perfect before our Heavenly Father. However, it doesn't make us immune from the suffering caused by our sins, but if we truly accept this offering of grace through faith, we can have eternal life with Christ Jesus. (Hebrews 10:14)

> . . . Because by one sacrifice he has made perfect forever those who are being made holy.

The longer men and women exist on Earth, the more sin will accumulate over the ages and the more suffering we will have to endure. However, we can never forget that Jesus has conquered sin and has promised that His strength in us will be sufficient for us to endure our sufferings. The following scripture is where we derive this promise even though it has a somewhat different meaning (referring to temptation instead of suffering), but God is faithful in all things. (1 Corinthians 10:13)

> No temptation has seized you except what is common to man. And God is faithful; he will not let you be tempted beyond what you can bear. But when you are tempted, he will also provide a way out so that you can stand up under it.

Faith and Works With Love

Most Christians claim to have accepted Jesus as their personal savior; but how do we really know that we have truly accepted Christ without just giving Him lip service? James tells us in Scripture that the truth of our acceptance in Christ is verified through our works. (James 2:20-24,26)

> You foolish man, do you want evidence that faith without deeds is useless? Was not our ancestor Abraham considered righteous for what he did when

he offered his son Isaac on the altar? You see that his faith and his actions were working together, and his faith was made complete by what he did. And the scripture was fulfilled that says, "Abraham believed God, and it was credited to him as righteousness," and he was called God's friend. You see that a person is justified by what he does and not by faith alone.

Yes, it is true that through faith we are saved by Christ's grace, but if we have sincerely accepted Jesus, the fruit of our faith will be seen in our works.

As the body without the spirit is dead, so faith without deeds is dead.

Jesus was clear when he addressed the importance of our faith to be put into practice. (Matthew 25:40)

Then the King will say to those on his right, 'Come, you who are blessed by my Father; take your inheritance, the kingdom prepared for you since the creation of the world. For I was hungry and you gave me something to eat, I was thirsty and you gave me something to drink, I was a stranger and you invited me in, I needed clothes and you clothed me, I was sick and you looked after me, I was in prison and you came to visit me.'

Then the righteous will answer him, 'Lord, when did we see you hungry and feed you, or thirsty and give you something to drink? When did we see you a stranger and invite you in, or needing clothes and clothe you? When did we see you sick or in prison and go to visit you?'

The King will reply, 'I tell you the truth, whatever you did for one of the least of these brothers of mine, you did for me.'

It is true that our works are corrupt and without first passing through the filter of Christ's precious blood, our works cannot be pleasing to God. However, the amazing sacrificial gift of salvation given to us from God does not make us unaccountable for our sins and should never be used as a means to justify them. Sin separates us from God and should be avoided at all costs. (Ephesians 2:8)

> *For it is by grace you have been saved, through faith—and this not from yourselves, it is the gift of God—not by works, so that no one can boast. For we are God's workmanship, created in Christ Jesus to do good works, which God prepared in advance for us to do.*

Scripture tells us that Christ will hold us accountable for our sins but He graciously allows us to be forgiven through confession. (2 Corinthians 5:10), (Galatians 6: 9-10), (Hebrews 10:26-31), (1 John 1:9)

> *Let us not become weary in doing good, for at the proper time we will reap a harvest if we do not give up. Therefore, as we have opportunity, let us do good to all people, especially to those who belong to the family of believers.*

> *For we must all appear before the judgment seat of Christ, that each one may receive what is due him for the things done while in the body, whether good or bad.*

> *If we deliberately keep on sinning after we have received the knowledge of the truth, no sacrifice for sins is left, but only a fearful expectation of judgment and of raging fire that will consume the enemies of God.*

> *If we confess our sins, he is faithful and just and will forgive us our sins and purify us from all unrighteousness.*

This can all be summed up with the following expression – "Actions speak louder than words." Good works help prove our love and faith in Jesus and are a witness to Christ's love in the world in which we live.

The Apostle Paul reminds us that love is the greatest of all. Love is a beautiful symphony of all the gifts combined into a harmonious expression of selfless giving. (1 Corinthians 13:4-7,13)

> *Love is patient, love is kind. It does not envy, it does not boast, it is not proud. It is not rude, it is not self-seeking, it is not easily angered, it keeps no record of wrongs. Love does not delight in evil but rejoices with the truth. It always protects, always trusts, always hopes, always perseveres.*
>
> *And now these three remain: faith, hope and love. But the greatest of these is love.*

Intercessory Prayer

Romans 8:26-27

> *In the same way, the Spirit helps us in our weakness. We do not know what we ought to pray for, but the Spirit himself intercedes for us with groans that words cannot express. And He who searches our hearts knows the mind of the Spirit, because the Spirit intercedes for the saints in accordance with God's will.*

It is comforting to know that the Holy Spirit fervently prays on our behalf. To me this is the most exciting aspect of prayer. How fortunate we are, especially in difficult times, to know that we have a wonderful advocate who knows exactly what to pray for in any situation. It is a mystery beyond our comprehension and one that touches God's inner most being. The Holy Spirit is love in its purest form and we are privileged to partake in it. This form of prayer has probably touched my life more than any other. It's usually most noticeable when I'm not praying at all but am in serious need of it.

Breakdown

Back when I was in high school, I went through a period of depression after having a huge argument with my girlfriend and one evening it all came to a head. I remember feeling terrible so I drove off to one of my favorite hunting spots just outside of town. It was already dark when I arrived and I pulled off the road and started weeping uncontrollably. My situation kept getting worse by the minute and felt I was on the verge of an emotional breakdown.

About that time, I felt the sudden urge to drive up to a local mountain only a few miles from where I was. This mountain was accessible by a steep windy road with a number of lookouts that had views of the city lights below. I hadn't been up that road for a while and wondered where this urge was coming from. Reluctantly, I wiped off the tears that had drenched my face and started driving towards this destination. The tears kept coming which made driving very difficult and I was fortunate to arrive safely.

I parked at a lookout near the edge of a vertical drop-off and my condition only worsened. While lying there on the front seat of my truck, on one of the worst days of my life, I noticed blurry headlights coming towards me. A truck pulled up next to me and I heard someone getting out. I got up from the bench seat now wet from my tears and began to panic even more when I realized who it was. It was my sister and dad walking towards me and there I was, a mess with no way to cover it up.

My sister knocked on the window so I pretended to be asleep. She then asked if I was alright and I finally acknowledged her with a weak yes. When I looked up, I saw the shocked look on my dad's face, staring at me in disbelief. He had never seen me so miserable and I was extremely embarrassed. My sister knew that I wasn't doing well because only an hour before, a strong inner voice told her to go up to the mountain by a lookout, where she had been before, and would find me in trouble. She immediately informed my dad that I needed help so they quickly headed up the mountain. I asked her how they found me and she broke out in tears while revealing her account. Dad just stood there silent, not sure what to say. Their presence helped to ease my pain and they talked me into following them home.

I don't know what might have happened if the Holy Spirit didn't send my sister to help me. I could have accidentally slid off the mountain because of my blurry, tear-filled eyes, or maybe it was as simple as God sending my sister and dad to help comfort me in my time of need. My sister told Dad all that had happened and I know now that this was just another seed planted for his later conversion. It meant a lot to me that God cared enough to comfort me.

Snow Angel

Another occasion occurred over two decades later when I was plowing snow early in the morning at a commercial parking lot. It was barely light and hardly a soul was out on the streets. Before backing up for another run, I caught a glimpse of a small green object in the snow. I stopped the truck and got out for a closer look. It turned out to be a twenty-dollar bill. "Wow!" I thought, but as I walked back to the truck, I saw something that made my heart almost pound out of my chest. There in the snow-covered parking lot, about ten yards behind my truck, was a young girl lying on her back making snow angels. If I hadn't seen the money, I might have backed right over her.

I asked myself what a young child was doing out there all alone playing in a commercial parking lot when it was barely light outside on a chilly winter morning. I went up and asked her where her mom was and she just smiled at me and shrugged her shoulders. I went back to my truck to call the police but just before I dialed their number, I looked back and she was gone. I searched diligently but she was no where to be found. I could only hope that her mom had picked her up when I had my back turned. The whole incident was really strange but I just praised our Lord for using the twenty-dollar bill to save the young girl's life. The Holy Spirit was definitely working overtime on behalf of the little girl. The thought of how close I came to running her over haunted me for days which kept reminding me how wonderful our Lord is for looking after all of us in our time of need.

† † †

The power of prayer in its many forms whether it originates from our minds, lips, or through our works should never be underestimated. With prayer, we have Christ's infinite power and hope. Without it, we have no relationship with God which leads to complete loss and despair. That is why it is so crucial that we pray before we act. The common expression often heard, "Now all we can do is pray," is at times completely backwards. God can solve any problem so it is only common sense that we should go to Him first. Because we are so stubborn, this is a hard habit to get into. However, once we put this into practice, the impossible becomes possible and the more we realize this, the better our lives will become. Our God is real and participates in every aspect of our lives. (Luke 18:27), (Mark 11:22-25), (Philippians 4:6-7)

> *Jesus replied, "What is impossible with men is possible with God."*

> *"Have faith in God," Jesus answered. "I tell you the truth, if anyone says to this mountain, 'Go, throw yourself into the sea,' and does not doubt in his heart but believes that what he says will happen, it will be done for him. Therefore I tell you, whatever you ask for in prayer, believe that you have received it, and it will be yours. And when you stand praying, if you*

hold anything against anyone, forgive him, so that your Father in heaven may forgive you your sins."

Do not be anxious about anything, but in everything, by prayer and petition, with thanksgiving, present your requests to God. And the peace of God, which transcends all understanding, will guard your hearts and your minds in Christ Jesus.

Chapter 8

Canadian Trip

The midsummer sun was hanging low over the horizon as we raced toward our destination still over 1,000 miles away. We had just passed through the Great Salt Lake Basin heading north and were climbing up into some gentle rolling hills, sparsely covered with sage brush and wild grasses. The vegetation was interrupted by vast expanses of green irrigated farm land with a few cows grazing off in the distance. Off to the right was an old abandoned farm house with several outbuildings and rusted farm equipment scattered in various places around the old homestead. With this in view, the surrounding landscape looked as if we were traveling at a time when the first settlers came west searching for a better life.

In the native fields, not yet disturbed by farming, we could still see remnants of the old wagon trails that had become eroded by time and were overgrown with a variety of ground covers. I wondered what was going through their minds as the pioneers slowly plodded along the dusty trail probably wondering what lie beyond the next hill or bend. We were traveling through this remote region at 75 miles per hour and if we blinked, something worth seeing would be missed.

I could picture a group of settlers gathered around a campfire after a long day's journey probably not singing songs but instead, completely exhausted. Some would be sick from dysentery or cholera while others would be injured from the hazards of the trail.

Our country has come a long way since the first settlers came west but I question if all our advancements have drawn us closer to God.

My family was on its way to my wife's parents' home located in British Columbia for a much needed break. The journey is long but there are many interesting sights along the way and seeing remnants of the Oregon Trail is one of them. Although there are areas that were not too scenic, the perspective while traveling at ground level cannot be beat. When flying at 30,000 feet everything below looks pretty much the same.

The sun had just set behind a distant mountain range leaving behind the classic fiery-red glow so typical in the semi-desert environment. We were still in Utah with the Idaho border quickly approaching. As soon as we crossed over the line, the scenery changed. There were fewer farm fields with more pinion, juniper, and cedar stands with vast expanses of sage brush and various wild grasses. It looked like we were in the middle of nowhere with only the interstate to remind us that we were not alone.

As we came around another bend, the irrigated farm fields appeared once again. Off in the distance I could see the flickering lights of radio towers perched high atop a ridge. As modern man continues to tame the old native environment, I couldn't help but to think of how beautifully quiet and desolate it must have been only a few hundred years ago back when only the bison, prairie dogs, coyotes, eagles, hawks, and other wildlife could be found, with the exception of Native Americans occasionally passing through.

On that day we had seen towering mountain peaks protruding well above timberline, colorful red rock formations with a few sandstone arches, beautiful lush river valleys, barren deserts, and majestic brush-covered mountains that seemed to lift right out of the level ground in order to gain a better view of the Great Salt Lake. We weren't even half way through our journey and already my mind, body, and soul were overwhelmed by God's incredible creation that He made for us to enjoy. With the exception of getting stuck in rush hour traffic in Salt Lake City and nearly being run over by an impatient semi-truck driver, our trip had gone remarkably well.

Problems Begin

Long trips can provide plenty of time to reflect on our lives which can unfortunately remind us of all the problems we face. For me, 2008 was one of the most challenging years of my life. On the other hand, 2007 was one of my best years. After only one week into the New Year (2008), problems started coming in from all directions. The worst was the loss of my health. Without warning, I awoke in the middle of the night and felt my heart beating extremely hard and fast. I remember feeling very weak and could hardly get out of bed to go to the bathroom. After finally standing up, my heart started pounding and while walking over to the bathroom, I noticed it was beating irregularly. This was a scary feeling that made me wonder if I was having a heart attack. I went back to bed and after several hours of worrying, I finally fell asleep.

The next morning I felt extremely weak and just lay in bed for several hours. When I finally got up, I felt a little better and headed for the shower. The weakness returned and as soon as the warm water hit my body, my heart started to thump irregularly again. This was the worst feeling I had ever experienced and it made me feel extremely vulnerable. For whatever reason, I started feeling better as the day progressed, but by evening my symptoms returned. It seemed to get worse at bedtime and as soon as I lay on my back, the heart palpitations returned. By standing up they would stop, but because I was so weak, I would have to sit down again which resulted in a vicious cycle. The rest of the night continued that way and by morning, I hardly slept a wink. My wife had had enough and demanded that I go the hospital and get checked out. I knew she wouldn't take no for an answer so I agreed to go. Why is it so hard for men to get help?

I was very weak and struggled to get ready to go to the hospital. On our way there, I started feeling better because my adrenalin kicked in. I told my wife all the things she would have to take care of if something happened to me. I couldn't believe I was talking that way – it all seemed like some sort of bad dream. When we arrived, I was afraid to go into the clinic for fear of what the doctor would tell me. My wife had to literally force me in there. After the usual waiting time I was finally attended to. I explained my symptoms and the nurse immediately hooked me up to an EKG machine which checked the electrical balance of my heart and could indicate if I had suffered a heart attack. To my relief, the test came out negative and everything looked normal with the exception of my heart rate which was at 98 beats per minute. The nurse then checked my blood pressure and found it to be slightly on the high side at 135/84. My usual rate is 110/70.

The doctor was then called in and he completed a quick exam and asked me to explain my symptoms. He then had the nurse test my pulse and blood pressure lying down, sitting up, and finally standing up. The results confirmed that while standing up my pulse was much higher than sitting or lying down. He concluded that I was severely dehydrated. He explained that when a person is dehydrated, the blood thickens because of the reduced water content making it much harder for the heart to pump. He also said the blood volume is reduced which also makes it extremely hard for the heart to pump efficiently. Simply put, my heart was struggling to pump the thick, molasses-like blood running throughout my body. He ordered a liter of IV solution to help re- hydrate my body and told me that I would feel like a new person after the treatment. I couldn't believe that something so simple would work so fast, but I was quickly proven wrong.

At first while receiving the IV, I started shivering violently and thought I was going to die but then the nurse informed me that she didn't have access to an IV warmer and had to administer them straight out of the fridge (definitely not a good idea). The cold water caused shock to my body. Despite the discomfort, the more fluid my body received the better I felt. Just like the doctor said, after my body finally warmed up, I felt almost completely normal after the treatment was finished.

It turned out I was so dehydrated that the nurse had to give me two liters of saline solution. She told me that usually after just one, most people have to relieve themselves. Before leaving, the doctor warned me to drink more water and told me that I could have died if I hadn't come in when I did. He gave me a prescription of six to eight glasses of water per day with a packet of electrolytes added in to help replenish my lost trace minerals. That I could handle – what a relief!

Later that day, I was still pinching myself thinking how simply my problem had been resolved. Looking back, I realized how I had become so dehydrated. That winter we were getting pounded by an unusual amount of snowfall and I was shoveling nonstop for myself and for my customers. Along with the high snow levels, the temperature was around zero degrees Fahrenheit so I never felt like drinking water while working. The doctor told me that dehydration can set in faster in extremely cold conditions than it can in hot weather. He claimed the cold dry air robs you of your moisture as evidenced by the vapor seen coming out of your lungs every time you exhale. Also, because it is cold, you don't feel like drinking as much as you would in hot weather. I never gave it much thought before but now I will definitely pay more attention.

† † †

Later that evening, I was still a little nervous to lie down because the heart palpitations from the two previous nights were still fresh in my mind. I decided to get it over with and lay straight onto my back which proved to be a bad mistake. My heart instantly started to palpitate so I jumped up out of bed and it stopped beating irregularly. This was disheartening because I thought my problems were over. Anxiety started settling in and my body went into high alert the rest of the night. This vicious cycle went on, over and over and left me with little or no sleep.

The next morning, I called the hospital and explained my situation. The doctor told me to try sleeping on my right side because that position would have the least amount of pressure applied to the heart. He told me that my heart may still be irritated from the effects of dehydration. He went on to explain that once the heart beats irregularly it can continue for awhile especially if the electrolyte minerals have been depleted such as magnesium and potassium. After hearing that, I quickly went to work on the internet looking for the best way to heal my body. I found out that once magnesium levels are depleted it can take months to restore them. Just because blood work shows a normal level doesn't always tell the correct story. Most of our magnesium is stored at a cellular level in the bone and soft tissues and only about 1% is stored in the blood.[25]

Several weeks had passed and the heart palpitations increased. At first they only came on while lying down but later they started occurring during the day while sitting and standing up. On one occasion, it got so bad that I went to the doctor's office while having them and they caught it on the EKG. To my surprise, the doctor told me not to worry about it and said he sees this on a regular basis. I asked him what I could do about it and he told me there was nothing that would help. He tried to comfort me by telling me that it wasn't life threatening and I would just have to get used to it.

This was not what I wanted to hear. I left the office frustrated and even more determined to find some answers. I had the EKG records forwarded to a local cardiologist that examined them and later

---

25 "Magnesium ." Office of Dietary Supplements, NIH Clinical Center, National Institutes of Health NIH , 30 Jan. 2005. Web. 28 Sep. 2008 <http://ods.od.nih.gov/factsheets/magnesium.asp>.

informed me that he didn't see anything that looked potentially harmful and told me to come in if the symptoms persisted.

† † †

I was determined to get my body back into good health and was willing to do anything to accomplish this. After further research on my own, I came up with a regimen of food and dietary supplements that I decided to stick to for the long term. My mom is a registered dietician so I also sought her help on a regular basis. I found that a powdered magnesium product that dissolved in warm to hot water worked best for my condition. I also dramatically changed my diet and eliminated high fat content and processed foods. Through trial and error I discovered that by eliminating processed sugars and wheat, the indigestion that always accompanied my heart palpitations was eliminated. Because of this, I switched over to a gluten free diet even though I am not wheat and gluten intolerant.

This was the first time I had lost my health and I wasn't about to sit back and do nothing. Instead, I declared an all out war. In order to eat better I alternated my regular cereal every morning with a nutrient-rich breakfast that was recommended by my mom. It consisted of scramble eggs (egg whites only if you have high cholesterol) cooked with flax seed, garlic, and freshly ground pepper. I thoroughly mixed in chopped lean meat (pre-cooked), tomatoes, green peppers, broccoli, asparagus, and finally mushrooms (all organic). I topped it off with a sprinkle of shredded low fat cheese. For a side dish, I occasionally toasted two corn tortillas and added a low fat (no cholesterol) buttery spread while hot and sprinkled on a generous amount of cinnamon over the entire surface. Served warm, I felt this was a delicious breakfast and still enjoy eating it today.

† † †

After a week went by, to my great relief the heart palpitations stopped! I still had a slight pressure feeling in my chest and upper abdomen, especially after eating a meal. My mom explained that it could be due to my radical change of diet because my body was still trying to adjust to the new food intake. I can almost certainly attribute the magnesium for helping stop the heart palpitations. After drinking a cup of warm to hot water with one tablespoon of magnesium mixed in, I instantly felt relaxed especially when taken before bedtime. Having made progress was a good feeling and I thanked Jesus for helping me with this problem. The heart palpitations only reoccurred a few more times and only when I was under a lot of stress.

Looking back, there were a lot of other problems going on that helped to intensify my health issues. The year started off with a tremendous amount of snow and ended up dumping over four feet. We usually get around one-foot of accumulation at the elevation where I live. Then at the beginning of the year, we were notified by an oil and gas company that they had plans to drill a new gas well right next to our property. This caused a lot of stress because it could threaten our health and safety and property value if not done properly.

Special Dog

Just prior to my health taking a turn for the worse, our dog ate a bunch of chicken bones and had to be taken to the vet. We were worried that she wouldn't survive when she started yelping in pain. This is no ordinary dog and my son considers himself lucky to even own her.

She is a beagle mix and was found by the human society roaming in a parking lot at a busy shopping center. My wife and son, who had been checking often, went to the pound to see if any new dogs had been brought in. Sure enough, there she was trapped behind bars eager to greet them with a wet kiss. My son instantly fell in love with her so they called me at work to come and see her. It was love at first sight for me as well so I gave my son the go ahead to claim her. She was on a seven-day hold before anyone could take her home and the time spent waiting for that day was torture for my son.

The day finally arrived and he woke up early to get there as soon as possible. They planned on arriving before it opened because they knew how popular she was and expected a lot of people to come for her. When they arrived, no one was there yet to my son's great relief. He quickly jumped out of the car and placed himself in front of the locked door ensuring that he would be first in line when they were due to open in an hour. Awhile later, an employee walked out and asked him if he was waiting for a dog and he nodded yes. He then asked if it was the beagle. My son smiled so big that he could hardly respond with another yes. The man told him there was a long list of applicants for this dog but it's usually first come first serve as long as he qualified. This gave my son some hope. He had prayed a long time for a good dog and it appeared his prayers would soon be answered.

Just before the pound opened, an older couple showed up who also wanted the beagle. About that time the doors were unlocked and the worker came out and told them there were five applications for her. He then informed the older couple that he would interview my son first since he was there before them. Shortly afterward, he reviewed the older couple's application and within moments, the worker awarded the beagle to my son. After hearing this, the older woman started crying. My son felt sorry for her but the excitement of his new dog quickly overshadowed any bad feelings. We have all become very attached to her and she has become a special part of our family.

That is why we were all so stressed out when our dog ate the chicken bones. The vet told us that she would have died if we hadn't taken her in. The $500 spent was well worth it to see her have a full recovery.

† † †

During this time period, two of my extended family members were having problems so I tried to help them out which also proved to be very stressful. A short time later while still recovering, I received more work then I could handle due to all the damage caused by the high snow levels. More work is usually a good thing but it was difficult to perform due to my compromised health. A month later, we took my wife's car in to replace an intake manifold gasket. A few hours after dropping the car off, I received a call informing me that after finishing the job and while on their test drive, the engine threw a rod. We had to fight hard to get partially reimbursed and were forced to buy another car.

A month later, my son started getting bad dizzy spells and literally collapsed on the baseball field while at practice. This problem went on and off for months until finally a nurse practitioner thought she found the cause that a GP and an ears, nose, and throat specialist failed to diagnose. She thought he may have a remote sinus infection that was difficult to detect and after spending nearly a half hour questioning and examining my son, she confirmed this. A dose of antibiotics seemed to cure him. Just prior to this, we were recommended to take him in for an MRI to search for a possible brain tumor. What a scary thought that was! We hoped the real problem was found.

Update – Vertigo Returns

In March of 2009 my son had two severe episodes of vertigo. He had done pretty well up to that point by preventing a sinus infection from occurring. But this episode was really bad. It was around 2:00 a.m. when I was awakened by a banging noise coming from our living room. I got out of bed to investigate. I found my son aimlessly wandering around, bouncing into the walls and furniture, coming dangerously close to hurting himself. I literally had to wrestle him to the ground because I thought he was going to injure himself. He kept yelling that the spinning sensation in his head was driving him crazy. This was disturbing to witness. I stayed with him until the out-of-control spinning sensation finally subsided allowing him to finally get some sleep. This was/is a scary thing to witness and we never wanted this to happen to him again. My wife came out and we both said, "Enough is enough!" We decided to take him to an out-of-town specialist to try and figure out what was causing our son to suffer. The next day he told me that I had over reacted and it wasn't as bad as I had thought. I probably did over react but it was frightening to see him in that state.

The earliest we could get him in to see a specialist was a month later. A short time prior to my son's appointment, he had another minor episode. We made the 400-mile journey with the hope that his problem could finally be diagnosed. They put him through a series of hearing and inner ear tests and concluded that his left inner ear had increased pressure. We informed them that my son had been in a severe car accident when he was younger in which he suffered a concussion. The doctor told us that a blow to the head could cause this type of inner ear injury. When we looked back at his medical records, it all started to make sense. We found he had been having dizzy spells since the car accident and there was no indication that this type of problem existed before it occurred. Now we at least knew where the symptoms were coming from.

The doctor went on to tell us that a low sodium diet with diuretics would help lessen fluid retention in the damaged part of the inner ear which causes the dizziness to occur.

After three days our son was doing much better. It was amazing that a low sodium diet could help our son get better that quickly. He has had a few minor episodes when he wasn't following his diet very well but as long as he stays with it, he does a lot better. It was a great relief for him and for us to finally figure out what was wrong and especially to find a solution to his problem. We thanked our Lord for this long-awaited answer. (**End of Update**)

† † †

Shortly afterwards, my wife's work started laying off employees and independent contractors right and left. She thought her contract would also be lost. Since she is able to work at home, this would have been a big deal because this was her largest account and those types of jobs are hard to come by. By the grace of God, it turned out that she didn't lose her contract but the stress of not knowing took its toll on an already stressful year.

Around that time, a small food shop that I helped get off the ground for a tenant started having problems. Originally it was set as a temporary shop to see if it would become established. Shortly afterward when things started looking positive, the tenant went to the city to apply for a permanent permit. They informed her that it would not be possible and then told her she would have to abandon her present location after the temporary permit expired in a few months. They had originally told her that becoming permanent wouldn't be a problem but later changed their minds. It cost us and the tenant over $20,000 to prepare the site and set up the shop, so a lot of money was at stake here. We both went to several city planning meetings and finally to the city council who ended up refusing to give her permanent status but did give her a one-year extension to find another location. To say the least it was stressful to think about.

Meanwhile, I was still dealing with my health issue and was making progress a little bit at a time. Though the palpitations were gone, I still had issues with pressure in the lower chest area and setbacks with the way I felt. By drinking plenty of water and eating on a regular schedule, I slowing regained my health. By the end of the summer, I had lost 25 pounds which was too much for my body height so my mom added healthier omega 3 fats to my diet which helped me regain a few pounds. My stomach and love handles lost most of their fat and I returned to my high school weight. It was amazing how fast it came off as soon as I stopped eating processed sugar and wheat. I would have stopped breathing air if it would have helped. I realized how important my health was. Without it, it is difficult to enjoy anything else – only our soul is more important.

Through it all, I kept asking God, "Why all the testing?" Was God preparing us for something in the future or was it just bad luck that would soon fade away as time moved forward? I found out that we weren't the only ones going through this period of testing. It seemed that most every Christian and secular person I talked to was experiencing extra problems that year. The problems we were going through paled in comparison to what some other people were telling me. However, this didn't take away from the fact that we were having a difficult time. I got so caught up with all the problems that I temporarily abandoned writing this book.

Despite all the trouble, God kept blessing my business with abundant work, almost double the average for a given year which helped pay for all the medical bills with money left over to put into savings. If work would have been slow on top of all the other problems, we would have been in real trouble. God promised that He would not allow us to go through more than we can handle, and once again, He was true to His Word. (Isaiah 41:10)

> Fear not, for I am with you; be not dismayed, for I am your God; I will strengthen you, I will help you, I will uphold you with my righteous right hand.

On the Road Again

We then traveled into a semi-desert region with sweltering temperatures over 100 degrees Fahrenheit. Looking out into the parched landscape from the climate-controlled environment of our vehicle, the only thing green and thriving was the vegetation being watered by pressurized irrigation systems. Everything outside this protective belt had long turned brown and appeared lifeless. Sometimes, I feel like that brown withered grass when I'm not spending enough quality prayer time with our Lord.

Almost appearing out of nowhere, the beautiful Snake River came into view. This massive river almost looked out of place in this semi-desert region. It was definitely the lifeline to the plant and animal species living there as well as the source of water for residents in the area. Just as the plant and animals depend on the Snake River for their source of life, we depend on God for everything in ours. God is our only oasis in the midst of troubles, and as Christians, trying to overcome all the obstacles in life is the challenge we face. Thankfully, everything is possible with Christ.

As we gradually climbed out of the Snake River Valley, the irrigated fields started to disappear and we started to get back into the native landscape of sagebrush and brown wild grasses. Fortunately for us, even when we are in dry periods in our own lives, God never abandons us even if it appears that He has. My sister inspired me with an analogy that really brought the above concept home. From her house, she can see a beautiful mountain peak off in the distance. The top of the mountain is sometimes obscured by clouds, only revealing its lower half. One day while in prayer, God inspired her with the following words:

> *Just because you cannot see the top of the mountain today does not mean it is not there. The same is true with Me, sometimes it seems I am not there but I always am. Have faith and believe and you will receive.*

I often think of this especially when going through dark times in my life.

Just as the scenery kept changing outside our car window, so do our lives – we have to keep adapting with God's help. We came over a small ridge and off in the distance was a beautiful, snow-covered mountain range. This was a refreshing surprise in the midst of the heat. We started to climb in elevation as we left the desert valley below and fir trees started to appear for the first time since leaving home. As the moisture levels and elevation increased, so did the variety of plant life. It is the same when we pray more – our life becomes more abundant, the way God intended it to be. The trees started getting thicker and soon developed into a mature forested region which was totally opposite the barren landscape we had left behind. If each prayer in our life represented one tree, how many barren hills could they cover in our lifetime?

After climbing up into the mountainous region, we descended down into the Columbia River Valley. We then crossed over the mighty Columbia River which was a spectacular sight to behold. Looking up stream we saw a dam that produced hydroelectric power. Watching the water being forced out of narrow passages was impressive, but even more so was the beautiful river that God had created. The river knows exactly where it is going as it gently winds its way down to the Pacific Ocean. Sometimes I wish I had that much sense of direction in my own life.

It had been a long journey so far with many sights to take in. We drove through another semi-desert region loaded with apple orchards and off in the distance I noticed a volcanic mountain peak protruding above the plains. We then began climbing up into the Cascade Range. At the summit, it had just finished snowing leaving a fresh coat on the trees and ground which was quickly melting. There was still plenty of snow remaining especially on the north facing slopes. This was unusual because it was midsummer. A thick fog covered the top of the peaks obscuring their grandeur. While coming down the west side of the mountain, we could feel the air start to thicken and warm as we descended into the Seattle, Washington, area. The highway was lined with large Douglas fir trees and it became evident that we were officially in the Pacific Northwest. The same look was prevalent throughout the rest of our trip with the addition of the beautiful Pacific Coastline occasionally visible along the way.

Just after sundown, we arrived at my wife's parents' house located in the Lower Mainland of British Columbia only a few minutes drive from the US border. In the summer months dusk lingers for several hours after sunset and at its peak, it doesn't get dark until after 10:00 p.m. We had a wonderful time reuniting with her family and had plenty of time to explore the beautiful coast lines and mountains that majestically rise above sea level.

† † †

We had some good conversations with my wife's parents. One topic was the high real estate prices for homes in the Lower Mainland of British Columbia and in certain areas of the United States and how home prices had exploded compared to prices in the mid to late 1900's. I explained how this was especially true in the western part of our country where owning a home even in a small town was becoming harder to afford, especially for younger people just starting out. They reminisced of the days not so long ago when they could buy a nice home in the Lower Mainland of BC for $40,000 and if they chose, a family could still comfortably afford to have the wife stay home to take care of the children. The same home today would cost over $500,000. We both agreed that it was very difficult for families in our present times. They explained how everything had become so congested in their area compared to past decades.

At that point in our conversation (referring to the high cost of living), I looked at my mother-in-law and asked her if she thought the best days were behind us. Without hesitation she replied, "I'm afraid so." I was somewhat surprised because this was coming from an eternal optimist. However, she also reminded me that it was all too easy to forget how tough the "good ole days" really were.

† † †

My mother-in-law grew up on a remote island located off the Vancouver Mainland. Her family lived in a small cabin with limited utilities. It consisted of a hand-dug water well and a wood burning stove for cooking and heating along with an outhouse for bathroom duties. Their boat was the only way to make it back to the mainland for supplies. If they got sick, they were pretty much on their own and if it was an emergency, they had to radio the police boat for help. If they needed extra food in addition to what was available on the island, it was up to them to go out and gather clams, oysters, and mussels from the beach, and hunt and fish for their meat. They lived a pioneer-like lifestyle and her father was quite the frontiersman. Because he was a land surveyor by trade he had several lakes and mountains named after him (Musclow Lake, Musclow Lake Trail, and Mt. Musclow, Tweedsmuir Provincial Park, British Columbia, and Musclow Lake, Ontario).

Her family went through many hardships back then but even with all the modern conveniences in her present day life, my mother-in-law still considers them some of the best days of her life.

My father-in-law's story is much different than hers but still quite compelling. He was born and raised in Italy. His father was killed in World War II which required him to quit school at an early age to help provide for his family. He quickly learned a trade as a barber and in his teen years immigrated to Canada with his mother and two sisters in search of a better life like so many others did in that era. Immigrants in Canada integrate differently than in the United States. In the US, cultures are usually absorbed into mainstream society, hence the term "melting pot." In Canada, however, their cultures tend to remain intact and continue on with their traditional heritages, thus the term "mosaic."

After meeting each other by chance (my mother-in-law's regular hairdresser had to cancel her appointment so my father-in-law had to cover) they developed a relationship and were soon married. He and his new wife were able to build a successful hair salon business and were blessed with four wonderful daughters.

Their stories are fascinating and they made me realize how much more material wealth we have compared to past generations – but has it really made us any happier? That is why it is so important to put Christ first in our lives. Even if darker days are ahead, we have the hope of Heaven to look forward to and more importantly, we have an almighty God who has promised to get us through our trials. God is our mountain and Jesus provides us with life giving waters. This is our hope and faithfully following His commandments is the only path that will bring us true joy. However, if we continue to rebel against God, our world will continue to plunge into darkness and will ultimately destroy itself through its own sin. I pray that we will wake up before it is too late and may God's power and mercy give us the strength to do this.

Chapter 9

Financial crisis of 2008/2009

It is now several months later in the fall of 2008 and I finally had an opportunity to work on this book again since coming back from our Canadian trip. It is amazing what can happen in just a few months. The last time I worked on this, real estate was at an all- time high along with gas prices over $4 per gallon. Almost out of nowhere, the world has plunged into an economic crisis and according to our President, it is being compared to the Great Depression of the 1930's. The first thing that came to my mind was the greed for money and our lust for more material things have finally caught up with us. The recession part wasn't a surprise but how quickly it engulfed us was.

It appears that the present crisis has resulted directly from corporate greed, lack of government oversight, and from citizens living above their means. Our government leaders and banking institutions contributed by deliberately loosening underwriting guidelines that allowed too many people to buy homes and other material goods they really couldn't afford. Many large banks could not resist the huge profits they were making which caused some to turn a blind eye to good underwriting practices. This has now come back to haunt them.

In my opinion, it was the high price of fuel that set this domino effect into motion. This in turn, made all the other products and services more expensive. People were already leveraged too high with debt and all it took was an unexpected increase in the cost of living to break the camel's back. The best road map out of this crisis is to follow God's Word. It is never too late to come to Him, no matter how much trouble we're in. But we must do our part and start living within our means – not according to our own desires.

It appears our government is trying to figure out a way to recreate the spending frenzy that got us into this mess in the first place. They, like many others, have become dependent on all the money it produced. Our economy relies too heavily on excessive debt levels. The more debt we get into, the better the indicators look because more material goods are purchased. This is a suicide train running out of control and it looks like our train has left the tracks, straight off a cliff.

The Commerce Department released statistics showing that consumer spending fell 0.5% and the savings rate increased by 3.6% in December of 2008.[26] Some economists complained this would slow down any recovery because people were starting to save their money instead of buying more goods and services. This is true if we are only looking out for our short-term interests, but this type of thinking is a disaster for the long-term economic stability of our country.

This is how backwards our economic system has become. It has made the survival of government and businesses too dependant on excessive spending by consumers. Notice also that we have been labeled as "consumers" and therefore, we are treated like a commodity instead of human beings. Don't get me wrong, I am very much in support of a balanced capitalist system, but I also

---

26 "Personal Income and Outlays, December 2008." Bureau of Economic Analysis, National Economic Accounts U.S. Department of Commerce, 2 Feb. 2009. Web. 28 Feb. 2009 <http://www.bea.gov/newsreleases/national/pi/2009/pdf/pi1208_fax.pdf>.

understand that if we do not honor Christian principles in our economy, we will become our own worst enemy with failure as the probable outcome.

This economic crisis can be likened to the comparison between a parasite and cancer. Our government and the economy feed off consumers, like parasites. Parasites will usually only take enough from its host to ensure its own survival but not enough to kill it. If the host starts to die, the parasite will back off a little allowing the host to regain its health. It does this knowing that its own survival is completely dependent on the host's. Cancer on other hand is not as smart as the parasite because it has no self control and eventually kills itself by killing the host. Unfortunately, I think we have gotten to the point where our parasite has turned into cancer. If there is any common sense left in our country, it is time to revive the host before it is too late.

In my opinion, the government needs to focus more on its citizens rather than on corporations. After all, isn't it the citizens who ultimately provide the government and corporations with their necessary funds to operate? Those who were laid off, including small business owners who do not qualify for any form of unemployment insurance, need help now. This includes providing direct help to homeowners who need to restructure their loans to avoid foreclosure. I know this isn't possible in all cases but it is better than only giving it to the banks and other large corporations that are supposed to be professionals and should have known better. Instead of trying to push people into more debt to help revive the economy, we should be setting up programs to help citizens, businesses, and governments to become better stewards of their money.

As more and more people become affected by this crisis, we need to make sure we have money available at the local, state, and federal levels to help people in need. If we are fortunate enough to quickly come out of this crisis but don't learn any lessons from it, we will plunge into a much deeper depression down the road. I personally think our nation will rally out our present dilemma, at least temporarily, within a year or two. The thing that I am worried about is the next recession/depression. I feel that one will prove to be catastrophic if we do not purge corruption and our wasteful spending habits.

I regret to say it but what we really need right now is a compassionate recession, not too different from the one we are going through now that will help wean us off our addiction to debt. The difference being, in the compassionate recession we would focus more on eliminating the root problem instead of trying to sustain an unhealthy economy as we are in our present crisis. We are like the alcoholic or the drug addict who has to go through withdrawal symptoms before overcoming their addiction. Our present economic recession could be used as a tool to help bring us back to a sustainable level. The process would be painful, but if we help one another we can get through it and come out of this much healthier in the long term. Our churches, government, businesses, and private citizens need to band together and set up various safety nets for those most affected.

It is time to change, especially if we are Christian. Scripture is clear when telling us to avoid unnecessary debt and not become too attached to worldly things. If we continue down the path of overt materialism, it will destroy our joy and lead only to our own spiritual and economic bankruptcy. For many that are secular, the above words will be laughed at, but as Christians, we have no excuse because we have been given the answers through Scripture that are necessary for us to weather out the storm. Serious events are taking place in the world and in our own personal lives – it's time to renew our faith and become steadfast in our convictions.

Unfortunately, the world probably won't follow God's advice in this crisis and the same failed policies will be repeated over again. If we listened to God and were fortunate enough to stay out of unnecessary debt, this crisis will not destroy us. On the other hand, if we failed to listen to Him, or events beyond our control caused us to accumulate large sums of debt, there is still hope, but it will require a complete change in our lives. We cannot do this on our own strength but will need help from God, family, and our brothers and sisters in Christ. In other words, we need to suck it up, bite the bullet, take our licks, or whatever else is necessary to get us back to a level that won't stress out our families by placing them in unnecessary debt.

Stock Market

As Christians, we need to seriously considering the choices we make before investing in the stock market. It isn't good enough to rely only on a stockbroker to choose our investments. We have ethical and spiritual obligations to research every company we invest in to make sure they are economically sound, and most importantly, do not support anti-Christian values. This is a lot easier to do in our generation with the wealth of information available to us using online research tools. No matter how much we like the company or how good the investment may be, we cannot allow ourselves to compromise our faith for money.

I recently had to sell a stock when I found out the company heavily contributed to organizations that support abortion. I sold it for a small loss and a few days later the stock went up over 100 percent. That was painful to watch and I felt like I was being punished for selling it. Life doesn't seem fair at times but I just have to keep reminding myself that Godly principles are more important than extra money. I also have to realize that He will more than make up for my losses with treasure in Heaven.

It's not always easy to follow God and without a consistent prayer life, it's nearly impossible. The strength of our faith is directly proportionate to the amount of prayer we have in our lives. As Christians, we have to be willing to spend time on our relationship with Christ even when it seems like it isn't doing any good. I know in my own life, there have been times when it appeared that God had either gone on vacation or really didn't care about my situation. My soul knows this isn't true but my flesh is weak and sometimes gets the best of me. This happens most often when I have neglected my prayer life.

I realize it would be impossible to find a perfect company to invest in free from any type of sin, but we must still strive to seek out investments that are not contrary to the core principles of our faith. This also applies to anything else we do in our lives including what type of companies we choose to buy our goods and services from. This is the challenge we face and one that will only become more difficult to overcome as the world continues with its downward plunge toward secular immorality. A steadfast commitment to God is our only hope.

Just like in baseball, it is time to step up to the plate and ask ourselves who we really are and what we stand for. To be a steadfast Christian, playing the middle ground won't work, just like swinging a baseball bat without conviction will cause a batter to strike out. It is either a full commitment or don't show up at all. This is exactly what I tell my players before a game and it is precisely what I and other Christians need to follow. The enemy is fully committed to its cause and will soon overwhelm us if we do not take this threat seriously enough to drastically change our lives.

God is counting on us in these end times to be His courageous followers. He wants us to be a shining light to a world that is consumed in darkness. Fixing our eyes on heavenly treasure should be our goal in life and until we are willing to put God first, we will not find true happiness. That is why we have to be willing to give up everything in this world. By doing so, we really won't be giving up anything because God will give us everything we need and more. This can only be accomplished through prayer. Pray hard, pray long, pray unceasingly, pray strong.

Government Bailouts

In the meantime, our government has created two huge bailout packages that will ultimately distribute trillions of dollars to themselves, corporations, and other financial institutions with the hope that it will create more jobs and will encourage banks to start lending money again despite the huge credit risk involved.

In my opinion, this will only be a short-term fix that will cause others to go further into debt at a time when we should be finding ways to get out of it. I feel these bailouts are a classic example of government bailing out those with power and influence while the small guy gets left out. It is disheartening to see that the common citizen will hardly get any direct help. By the time these funds filter through the inefficiencies of our government and corporations, it will amount to pennies on the dollar for us. Currently, the latest bailout bill has only set aside a $500 deduction for a single filer yet they have set aside trillions for themselves and corporate interests. Beside the point, how does our government think they/ we are going to pay for this? This is nothing more than a ball and chain strapped around ours and our children's necks. If it doesn't bankrupt us first, it will take generations to pay it back. Where's the common sense here?

I'm not blaming this on any one individual because I understand it's just the way our whole system works (spend now, pay later). Nobody wants to be left holding the bag so politicians scramble to at least temporarily fix the problem so it doesn't self destruct on their watch. We know why they do it but wouldn't it have been better to save our resources to deal with the known problems as they occur rather than trying to speculate on the unknown that may never occur? The fact that we work so hard for our money makes it extremely frustrating to see our tax dollars potentially mismanaged. I can only pray that this will come out better than expected, but right now it doesn't look too promising.

This huge bailout package reminds me of a gambler that puts all his/her money on one pull of the slot machine in hopes of winning the big one. You wouldn't call in an aircraft carrier to rescue someone who has fallen off a small fishing boat; instead, you would throw them a life preserver. It also wouldn't be wise to use the space shuttle to drop off food supplies to people suffering from a natural disaster; a cargo transport plane would be a more logical choice specifically designed for the task at hand. Each item in this bill should have been thoroughly scrutinized to ensure that it was specifically targeted to immediately address the crisis at hand. Unfortunately, the bailout package was so large that many congressman and senators didn't even have time to read it all before voting. This was one of our nation's most important decisions and some of them didn't even take the time to read it! How disappointing is that.

Grandpa and Grandma Living in the Great Depression

As stated earlier, our leaders have compared this economic crisis to the Great Depression of the 30's. I think this has been used, at least in part, as a scare tactic to help get their bailout packages passed. Who knows, maybe the situation is worse than I realize, but after hearing stories from my grandparents about the real Great Depression, this one so far seems pale in comparison.

Grandpa told me he had become so desperate for work during that time he had no choice but to leave home to look for it. There were rumors of jobs available in the Chicago area so he decided to leave his home town in the rural Western United States and travel to the big city. According to Grandpa, he didn't have enough money to catch a bus so he jumped from train to train like a hobo to reach his destination. When he finally arrived, he was tired and hungry and was willing to take on any job he could find. Grandpa's dream of opportunity quickly changed when he was faced with the reality of long food lines and people struggling to find work on a massive scale.

Despite all the hardship, he managed to find a dirty job installing insulation in a large industrial tower. From there, he went from job to job until he finally realized he wasn't doing any better than he was at home. While hitchhiking on his way to the rail yards in hopes of catching a free ride back home, a car pulled over to give him a ride. After climbing in, Grandpa noticed the driver was well dressed and appeared to be weathering out the Depression in good fashion. He got up the courage to ask the man what he did for a living and the man went on to tell him that he worked for an organization that he couldn't talk about. Grandpa bluntly asked him if had anything to do with the Mafia and the man didn't respond. Being somewhat desperate at the time, he then asked the man if he could get him a job and the man suddenly broke his silence and told him to never ask that question again.

After pulling over a short distance from the rail yards, Grandpa thanked him for the ride and he went on his way. He thought it was Al Capone himself. I never believed it was really Al Capone but just went along with it. Regardless, this encounter really made an impression on Grandpa and he repeated this story to us on numerous occasions.

Upon arriving back home he took on various employment and was finally able to land a good paying job as a locomotive machinist. During that time period, he had to check into the hospital to undergo surgery to repair a hernia. Later while recovering, he met his future wife who happened to be the nurse taking care of him. There was a baby screaming uncontrollably near his room so Grandpa asked her if he could hold the child to quiet the infant down. She and another nurse just laughed at him but his insistence prevailed so they brought the baby to him. The infant immediately stopped crying and they were amazed. This really made an impression on Grandma. Grandpa took full advantage of it by quickly asking her out on a date which led to their engagement and later marriage.

Grandma is one of 16 children who grew up on a fruit farm in the Desert Southwest. It was sad to learn that seven of her siblings died at or near child birth. Her parents instilled in them strict biblical principles which laid the foundation that enabled her to survive in tough times. Today, like many others in her generation, she still cuts napkins in half and acts like she is poor even though she really isn't. Yet, she has always been generous with her time and money. She was always the one that took me and my siblings on fun adventures such as raft trips, hiking, skiing, and camping and actively participated as well. Because of her fun-loving nature, everyone who met her fell in love with her. She is now in her nineties and is still doing quite well.

The Great Depression was so harsh that it changed people's lives forever. I sincerely hope and pray that our present crisis will not see the epic proportions of unemployment, poverty, and loss of hope experienced in the past.

Good Intentions

Many government leaders including both Presidents Bush and Obama had good intentions with these bailouts. However, it appears their focus was mainly on the present with less emphasis on the future. But is it really fair to pass trillions of dollars of debt onto our children just so we can have short-term relief? I personally think we would have been better off if we had just taken our licks and gotten it over with. All we have done at best is buy some time but we haven't addressed the root cause of the problem. Instead of spending more money on material things, we need to start spending more time, talent, and treasure on things that really matter. Our government and businesses would also do well by implementing the principles clearly set forth in Scripture.

If we follow Jesus, we will get through this recession without losing our spiritual wealth which is the most important. When the secular world sees that we are still joyful despite all the problems around us, they will want to find the source of our happiness. This will open up an opportunity to witness Christ's love to them. If on the other hand, we follow the world into panic, there won't be anyone to lead the way. It is a comforting thought to know that as the world plunges into crisis, Christians can still rejoice because we do not rely on the things of this world for our well being; rather, we draw our strength and joy from our mighty God. The sooner we realize this, the better our lives will become. (Hebrews 13:5)

> *Keep your lives free from the love of money and be content with what you have, because God has said, "Never will I leave you; never will I forsake you."*

Why Are We Being Tested?

Now I partly understand why my family and so many others have been tested this past year. God has been preparing Christians by gently shaking us out of our worldly trance by allowing difficult situations in our lives to bring us closer to Him. This year my life started out similar to last with the exception of a few major things. My health is much improved but my work load has been significantly reduced from the previous year. However, I'll trade better health for less work any time.

Our dog re-injured herself by jabbing a stick deep into her leg, but after paying a $300 vet bill she'll be fine. As already explained, my son had a relapse of his sinus infections and associated dizziness and we scheduled him to see a specialist in the spring. The gas company once again started to renew their interest in drilling a new gas well near our home which has caused a lot of stress. However, we are working on a solution that will hopefully turn out better than expected. Meanwhile, the world has plunged into a severe recession and how bad things will become is anyone's guess. One thing is for certain – if we have Jesus in our hearts, we will never be abandoned no matter what the circumstances. But do we really believe this promise from Christ? And if we say yes, are we willing to do whatever it takes to live a steadfast Christian life in a world gone astray?

Financial Update 1

Three months into 2009, things keep getting worse. The financial system is literally falling apart even though the government continues to spend billions of dollars in bail out money. The more Washington does to try and slow it down, the worse it appears to get. More and more financial scandals keep popping up revealing the massive amount of corruption that helped contribute to this financial collapse. It has been troubling to see so many large companies that have been around for years going out of business. Foreclosures continue to escalate and people are losing their jobs at an alarming rate. This is starting to look more and more like the real thing. It appears that no matter how hard the government tries to spend us out of this, the economy continues to struggle. The market is just going to have to correct itself which could prove to be very painful for our nation and the world.

Pro-life Concerns

Despite all the problems, President Obama has recently proposed to lift the ban set by President Bush on embryonic stem cell research. While campaigning for president in July 2007, Obama also made a promise to Planned Parenthood that the first piece of legislation he would sign would be the Freedom of Choice Act.[27]

This bill would overturn pro-life laws and could make abortion on demand a national right that government would enforce throughout our country. To enact the Freedom of Choice Act could also make abortion procedures mandatory in faith-based hospitals regardless of their religious convictions. This could also require taxpayers to fund abortions against their will.[28]

As discussed in Chapter 5, we are all accountable to God and will have to justify everything we do in life, including our voting

27 "Fight FOCA." Americans United for Life Action (AUL) N.p., 2008.
   Web. 24 Sept. 2009 <http://www.fightfoca.com/>.
28 "Fight FOCA." Americans United for Life Action (AUL) N.p., 2008.
   Web. 24 Sept. 2009 <http://www.fightfoca.com/>.

records. Trying to convince God that abortion is acceptable will not be an easy task. Abortion is contrary to everything He stands for. Unfortunately, many of us were caught up in all the excitement and were fearful for our finances and it appears we chose to vote from our wallets instead of our hearts. During the recent election, a large number of pro-choice representatives, including our President, were voted in. It's too bad that President Obama isn't pro-life. He has the personality, smarts, and charisma to be an excellent leader if only in the right direction. He has a gifted tongue unlike anyone we have seen since President Ronald Reagan. I am definitely not trying to take away from the fact that he is the first black president. Rather, this is a wonderful testament to the progress we have made in our country. I will support President Obama in any way possible as long as it doesn't go against what I believe. My personal preference would have been for Alan Keys to be the first, mainly because of his passionate moral convictions. Unfortunately, his campaign fell short but his words will not be forgotten.

Furthermore, this has nothing to do with the color of someone's skin or the party in which they are affiliated. Instead, it has everything to do with our Christian principles. I will pray for President Obama and encourage others to do the same that he will have a change of heart. Some are saying that anyone who objects to Obama's policies on abortion is a racist. In my case and with many others, this simply isn't the truth. Abortions are performed on both Caucasian and minority pre-born babies. Pro-life supporters want all people to live no matter what their ethnic heritage may be. Every child is precious. We cannot expect God to help us if we continue to harm the unborn. Instead, things will only get worse and we will only have ourselves to blame. We may soon experience temporary relief from our present economic crisis but unless we change our misguided ways, the problems will return and only intensify. **(End of update)**

Financial Update 2

Several weeks later, the market seems to have at least temporarily bottomed out and has started to recover a bit although unemployment and foreclosures continue to rise. Uncertainty and fear still grip our nation and the world. The financial crisis has been difficult but the level of intensity from ongoing personal trials has been even worse. Since the beginning of 2008 before the financial crisis even occurred, I could sense that something was in the works. I have heard this from both Christian and secular people. Never before have I personally experienced and witnessed so many problems. It makes me wonder if we are living in the times that Jesus prophesized about concerning a troubled time in history when even the elect will be deceived. Or is this just one of many warnings that will happen if we continue to live in our sinful ways?

For the past two years it feels like I have literally had the daylights beaten out of me and there have been times when I have come close to yelling out, "I surrender!" Having said that, I refuse to quit because I know deep down that it isn't through my own strength that victory will be achieved. Rather, I have to cling to the promises of Christ. His words do not waiver and can always be trusted, unlike those from the world. Because of His truth, I have the strength to keep reminding myself who is in control.

(2 Chronicles 20:15)

> . . . *The battle belongs to the Lord.*

Therefore, we are no match fighting this on our own. It is only through God's power and divine protection that we can survive this onslaught of evil. The challenges before us will not be easy and will take a level of commitment and faith on our part that is unprecedented. Thankfully, we do not have to do this on our own – we have a wonderful advocate through the Holy Spirit who will speak on our behalf and guide us through these difficult times.

Business leaders, government officials, employers, employees, common citizens – we all need to learn from our mistakes and try not to repeat what got us into this mess in the first place. We have to put our own selfish desires to rest and think about what is best for the present and future of our local communities, nation, and the world. If we claim to be Christian, we have to start acting like one now. The root cause of this crisis is not economic; rather, it is only a symptom of the real problem which is the moral collapse of society. Therefore, becoming steadfast in our faith is the only way we will have any long-term relief from our present trials. God will enable each one of us to endure these troubled times. He will also give us supernatural joy and peace even when the rest of the world lives in fear and anxiety. This can only be accomplished if we eliminate the distractions that take us away from Christ's will for us. (**End of update**)

Another Great Depression?

April has come and the financial situation has started to level off after a surprising 25% gain in the stock market in one month. Some analysts think the gains were only temporary and others can't predict the direction of the market due to its extreme volatility. While writing this, I am sitting in front of our window looking out at a wind-whipped sky that is so full of dust that it looks like we're living on Mars. I can't remember a time when it was this severe. It is an eerie scene that reminds me of stories I heard from Grandpa of the Dust Bowl years during the Great Depression.

In 1918 prior to the Great Depression, Grandpa lost his sister to the Spanish Flu. Hundreds of other people died from it in his hometown and millions died throughout the world. Now we have swine flu emerging which appears to be related. This is just one more iron in the fire we have to deal with. I often wonder if all the deaths caused by World War I in combination with the Spanish Flu might have been a contributor to the Great Depression, just as 9/11 on a lesser scale may have been partially responsible for our present financial crisis. It is hard to get my mind off our country's present situation.

The events preceding the last Great Depression have many similarities of those today. The Roaring Twenties changed a mostly conservative generation into one of crime, free sex, and partying all while enjoying economic prosperity. The same can be said of our generation which has far surpassed their evil behavior. Is there a connection here linking immoral behavior to economic hardship, and if so, will we ever learn from the mistakes of our past? The current crisis has taught me how quickly hard times can come upon us with little or no warning. That is why it is so important to always be alert and ready. The Scripture referring to a thief coming in the middle night is good advice to follow for any situation. (Luke 12:35-40)

> It will be good for those servants whose master finds them ready, even if he comes in the second or third watch of the night. But understand this: If the owner of the house had known at what hour the thief was coming, he would not have let his house be broken into. You also must be ready, because the Son of Man will come at an hour when you do not expect him.

A Brother and Sister Remember

I was recently talking to one of my customers who is 92 years old. She lives with her brother who is 91. The two of them are some of the nicest people I've ever met. They were both widowed over 20 years ago and decided not to remarry, but instead chose to live together to help with the bills and for companionship. I asked her if today's economic problems are worse than in the Great Depression and she and her brother just laughed. She then told me that it is nearly impossible to compare our present time with theirs. It was a completely different way of life, one that was much simpler and one where most people were more self sufficient than in today's world.

She went on to explain how her family scraped by, living off their livestock and planting crops. She was fortunate that her father was a veterinarian who put his trade to good use during hard times. When she first got married, she and her husband moved into an old barn with a large sliding door as the only entrance. There were no windows so her husband cut out a spot in the back wall and managed to find some glass to fill it. They moved into the barn because it came with her husband's job which was to take care of one hundred pigs for $30 per month pay. I asked her if that was enough back then to live on and she said, "Of course not! We had to scrape and pinch for everything we had. All our clothes were worn out and full of patches, one on top of the other."

She said all this with a big smile on her face so I asked her if she was happy during that time. Immediately she burst out, "We had the time of our lives even though things were tough. We opened up the barn on the weekends for community dancing and we danced well after midnight." While telling the story it was as if she and her brother were actually there, reliving their past. "Back then, we knew how to have fun with simple things that didn't cost any money. Today, everything has to be a major event before people are satisfied even if it gets them into debt – like with my daughter's family who does this on a regular basis. They spend more money on a single family trip than we do in an entire year."

I could see the change in her eyes as the joy turned into a more serious look. I then asked her if the Roaring Twenties were as bad as history made it out to be. They both jumped in and said, "It absolutely was! Women started to drink and smoke in public places and they started to wear short dresses for the first time. They also began cutting their hair." I was surprised to learn that women didn't cut their hair very often before that time period.

She also kept telling me how lucky she and her brother were to still be alive, especially since she just had a heart attack and her brother had recently undergone brain surgery. It was amazing how mobile she was and I joked with her that I would feel very fortunate to be in as good of shape as she was when I get that old. Older people have so much to offer if we will just take the time to listen to them. Upon leaving, I told them that we will have plenty of time to catch up on things when we're all in Heaven. They both just laughed nodding their heads in agreement.

She reminded me that in the tail end of the Roaring Twenties, our country and the world had plunged into the Great Depression which was quickly followed by a drought-ridden dust bowl which was then followed by World War II. Looking back, if you add everything up, it appears that God had judged our country back then for falling into moral disparity. Our generation is making the same mistake but in a more dramatic fashion and now we too have fallen into a "great recession." I hope the recent dust storms we have been experiencing are not a premonition of what's to come. I certainly hope and pray that a world war won't be the end result but that is exactly what we could be facing if we fail to learn from the mistakes of history. The world is in serious trouble if we do not repent and come back to the ways of our Almighty Father.

All we have to do is look back in history to see that unrepentant societal sin always brings on God's judgment. Fortunately for us, just as it was for Nineveh in the days of Jonah the Prophet, it is never too late to wise up and avoid impending disaster. But will we answer God's call to righteousness and abandon our evil ways? If not, God will have no choice but to chastise the world because he loves us too much to allow this kind of evil to continue. **(End of update)**

Update 3 – Trials Continue

It is now May 2, 2009, and my life continues to be full of difficult challenges which include coaching baseball, work, our property, our government, and within my own family. Problems are freely flowing to the point that it has become overwhelming. Like many of us, my sister has also been going through some hard times and while on a prayer line, the following Scripture was given to her from Job 5:12-18.

> *He thwarts the plans of the crafty, so that their hands achieve no success. He catches the wise in their craftiness, and the schemes of the wily are swept away. Darkness comes upon them in the daytime; at noon they grope as in the night. He saves the needy from the sword in their mouth; He saves them from the clutches of the powerful. So that the poor have hope, and the injustice shuts its mouth. Blessed is the man who God corrects; so do not despise the discipline of the Almighty. For He wounds, but He also binds up; He injures, but His hands also heal.*

In times of Job-like trials, we need Job-like Scriptures to help us overcome them. God not only protects the righteous from their enemies but He also gives the wicked a chance to redeem themselves because he is rich in mercy, "For He injures, but His hands also heal." I have been that wicked person more times than I would like to admit. His grace and mercy are what give me the hope that even a sinner such as myself can be accepted by God, even when the world rejects me. Having enough faith to truly believe in His Word is the great struggle I face on a daily basis and one that I will continue to battle the rest of my life. **(End of update)**

Update 4, May – August 14, 2009

I hardly know anyone who isn't facing Mt. Everest in their lives right now. The economic problems have been compounded by personal trials that have plagued Christians throughout our land. Health, financial, family, and social troubles are the story. These types of problems have always been around but it appears that things have intensified and continue escalating as if we were quickly hurling toward some type of climax or life-changing event yet to be revealed.

I know in my own life everything, except for my health, has taken a beating lately. Last year my work load was nearly doubled compared to an average year, and as already mentioned, my health was also at its worst during that time period. I remember thinking to myself, "I'd trade the extra work for better health in a heart beat." Well, what I asked for has come true. Today, my work is down over 60 percent from this time last year but my health is much improved – thank you Lord! Work is important but compared to my health there is no comparison. I know that God will take care of our needs as I've been down this road enough to know that He is faithful.

The first several months of this year, people closed their wallets for good reason. As the news started looking a little better, I finally started getting calls again. My work has been coming from customers that I did jobs for over ten years ago. I haven't talked to some of them since then but now, out of the blue, they are calling me for work to be done. I know this isn't a coincidence and can clearly see God's hand writing all over it. It has been like a customer reunion and has been fun catching up on everything since last seeing them.

My wife and I joked last year when all the jobs came pouring in that God must be preparing us for something. We had no idea that the economy would collapse so quickly. I rely on commercial work both in real estate and in general contracting and this market has really been hit hard in our area. If we were not so fortunate to be nearly debt free, we would have been in serious financial trouble right now. Thanks to God for adequately preparing us for this moment. We had to do our part through many years of sacrificing but now it has paid off. It still hasn't been easy but at least we won't lose our home.

We are, however, facing another problem with our property. As explained before, our county government recently changed the oil and gas rules making it easier for gas companies to drill new wells next to people's homes. Before the changes, we had a solid level of protection that prevented new gas wells from being drilled in close proximity to people's homes.

To make a long story short, I have become involved with a group of affected homeowners to try and persuade our county government to reinstate these lost protections. When the politicians said we need to drill more at home, they weren't kidding. I didn't realize that in our case it meant drilling a new gas well within 300 feet of our home. Don't get me wrong, I am for responsible drilling when people's health, safety, quality of life, and property values are not compromised, but find it completely unacceptable when government and the industry place profit over common sense and respect for citizens' rights. Infuriating homeowners is not a very wise PR campaign for the oil and gas industry to gain confidence and trust in the public eye.

The endeavor to protect our property has taken many hours of time and effort but slowly we are making progress, and at our last county commissioner meeting, planning staff informed us that after thoroughly examining our particular site, they would not allow a new gas well to be drilled next to our property. This was a complete reversal from what they had been telling us. I thanked them for the good news but informed them that I would still continue to work on this issue.

† † †

My grandma who is almost 91 has recently lost her tenant that ran a contract postal station for 25 years. The US Postal Service reduced the dollar amount of the contract to the point where it wasn't feasible any longer for the tenant to continue. The Postal Service has been hit hard during this crisis which has now affected Grandma who has lost nearly half her income. We will make sure she gets another tenant but it is hard to replace something that steady. It has been rough for all of us.

Our family business partnership is also losing a tenant who runs a small kiosk at the same location. In this case the tenant has been very successful, but the city planning department is forcing them to leave because they claim the tenant's small building looks too temporary in nature and doesn't meet present code. This is unfortunate because the city originally agreed to allow this business to set up shop year round, but now they have changed their minds after our partnership and the tenant have spent thousands of dollars to get the operation going. She petitioned to receive a variance but the city would not budge. This is a business that is flourishing and is very popular in our community. She received hundreds of petitions from loyal customers to allow her to continue operations at her present location. Despite the public backing, the city wouldn't budge even in a struggling commercial market. President Ronald Reagan's view on government being the problem in certain circumstances was correct in our situation.

Recently, I went inside Grandma's former post office building (now vacant) and laid my hands over the empty counter and asked God to help us find another good tenant. While I was praying, a person came in unexpectedly while my head was down and my arms were outstretched in prayer. I quickly jumped up and wondered if they saw me that way. If they did, I'm sure they thought I was a little crazy.

Tragic Loss of Life

On a more tragic note, one of my second cousins recently died from injuries suffered in a car accident on the way home from an out-of-town concert. Six teenagers, all around 18 years old, were on their way home when apparently the driver fell asleep in the early morning hours and crashed into a guard rail. Five of the passengers survived but my cousin wasn't so fortunate. It was a brutal tragedy especially for his immediate family. Why did he die when all the others survived? Thank God the others lived but sometimes life just doesn't seem fair. It is times like these that our faith in God becomes so important. Instead of becoming angry at our Lord, we have to embrace and trust Him even if we can't understand why bad things happen.

Even though I wasn't very close to my cousin, I cried more at his funeral than I did at my dad's. Seeing his parents and all the high school kids completely losing it with tear-filled eyes was more than I could handle. Some of the kids present didn't know our Lord so I prayed with all my heart that this unfortunate circumstance would help bring them to Jesus. I have a heavy burden in my heart for my cousin's parents and family members who are going through one of life's greatest hardships. Death is truly a saddening experience especially for those who are left behind. This was a wakeup call for how quickly life can be taken from us and how important it is to always be ready to meet our Lord.

> *Lord Jesus, please go with my cousin, let him be with you in Paradise. Comfort all those in their time of need. Take away their pain and replace it with your tender love. Amen*

Baseball Playoffs

Drastically switching the subject and on a more positive note, baseball had finally gotten on the right track and somehow we ended up with two of the best pitchers in our area. Our team consisted of seven high school players who made the junior varsity team and six players who were either cut from the high school team or didn't try out during the regular season. In other words, we had a good mix of players. Through the years, my assistant coach and I have picked up several players that other teams may not have considered. It has been very satisfying to watch some of these kids develop into solid players when others had given up on them. We ended up having moderate success by tying for fourth place in the regional state playoffs out of eight teams. It didn't help us any after we lost one of our catchers to swine flu. He contacted it while on vacation traveling abroad which forced him to quit our team toward the end of the season. He suffered with a fever over 102 degrees Fahrenheit for several days which gave him and his parents quite a scare. He ended up recovering and is now doing well. From what they told me, this is nothing to mess around with.

Last season despite our lack of overall talent, we made it to the final round of league playoffs and upset the only undefeated team in our division. The game turned out to be like something out of a movie. That night, we came together as a team and the players fed off each other like I've never seen before. The other opponent had the most talent, but like with most all-star teams, they weren't playing as a group but rather, each player for themselves. This was a team who had beaten us by 20 points in the regular season but our players working together were stronger than the opposing team's individual efforts, and that game proved it. One pencil is easy to break with your hands but if you try and break 12 pencils bundled together it becomes extremely difficult.

† † †

The strength of team work applies to all aspects of our lives whether it's in marriage, friendship, at work, at play, at church, or especially when our faithful service men and women courageously fight for our freedom. If only we would all learn to work together, our world would be a much better place. That is why I love the sport of baseball because if coached properly, it teaches qualities that are essential to a successful Christian life.

Right now there are thousands of families struggling, with some in the final innings just trying to hold on. As in baseball, we have to remember to keep a cool head and work together to overcome our difficulties. Most importantly, we have to remember to bring God into the equation especially with tensions at an all-time high in our world. For the first time in history, the definition of family and marriage are being redefined by the courts and not in the way God intended.

We are at a critical juncture and are in the bottom of the 9th inning getting pounded on all fronts by the opposition. The game we are in is a must win because it has eternal consequences. We are the players and God is the owner/manager and we have to listen and do whatever he tells us. Our rule book is the living Word of God and our prayers give us the inspiration and strength to carry on. His message is the clear path to victory if only we will listen to Him. We must reach down deep and give it all we have. We can't afford to wait for someone else to do it this time – it will take the efforts of all of us to help turn the tide that threatens the existence of our families and our Christian way of life.

Are Happy Days Here Again?

In August, I read a number of articles that proclaimed that happy days are here again. The Dow's large recovery over the past few months has some investors looking forward to recreating the good ole days of record breaking stock prices once again. But how can you go from the "great recession" of 2008/2009 to a good economy in a matter of a few months? If that really happened, we were all told a bunch of baloney. However, just because the Dow is going up now doesn't mean it won't fall again. The Dow reacted the same way during the Great Depression. And just because the stock market is going up doesn't mean the average citizen is benefiting.

The national unemployment rate is over 9% and home foreclosures are still on the rise. Until the housing and job markets stabilize, we will not have a true recovery. As I said before, I see the market recovering temporarily for a period of time (no clue how long it will last). But then the market will once again quickly collapse under its own weight of debt. I am not trying to be a gloom and doom prophet here but rather, it is only common economic sense. If you print trillions of dollars that you don't have, it will eventually catch up with you. Our government has pulled out all the stops to try and save our ailing economy with little left in its arsenal. Literally selling the family farm may give us short term relief but what price will we ultimately pay for this in the long run?

As long as citizens and governments are strapped with debt, we will be vulnerable to economic collapse. I pray that we won't have to go through more hardship, but as long as we continue to live contrary to God's principles I don't see how we can avoid it. If we are fortunate enough to have a solid recovery, it will be a period of grace from God that will give us time to get our finances in order. We have to start working on this now.

Regardless of the apparent short term revival in our economy, it is truly an amazing time with companies such as General Motors in part being bought up by our government to prevent them from going out of business. The government takeovers are the most disturbing to me.

What's going on and will it ever stop now that the monkey is out of the bag? Our country is becoming numb to all the changes and nothing seems to shock people anymore. Lately, however, people are starting to wake up and because of this, we are once again having "tea parties" throughout our land. This hasn't happened since the time shortly before our country was originally founded. Our country is quickly changing into something that most could not have imagined only a year ago.

It appears that some members of our government are also trying to take over healthcare. I'll be the first to admit that the cost of health insurance is out of control, especially if you're self employed. The Republicans recently had eight years to work on this but in my opinion, did little to help reform it. Now we are witnessing just the opposite where most of the Democrats want to take it over. Where's the balance? We need reform, not a complete takeover. Republican leaders need to quit complaining about this and come up with their own version before it's too late.

Rules could be put in place to require insurance companies to charge more reasonable rates and to accept more customers, especially those with pre-existing conditions. Generous tax incentives could be offered to those companies to help offset the higher costs associated with taking on more risk. Employees and the self employed should also receive larger tax credits to help offset their ever increasing premiums. A safety net needs to be put in place for those who really can't afford it.

The most dangerous part of a government-controlled healthcare system would be the probable funding of abortion, embryonic stem cell research, and the possible practice of euthanasia. This would require all taxpayers, whether or not they support these controversial issues, to pay for them. This would force pro-life supporters to go against their core beliefs and even worse, it would increase the number of abortions performed in our country.

Where will it stop and what will we become? Will we rally and come together as a nation or will we self destruct through our own pride and arrogance? The stakes are high, our future uncertain. As Christians, we must stay grounded to our faith in Christ who has already triumphed over all the wickedness of the world. God is our strength now just as he was in King David's time. (Psalm 46:1)

> God is our refuge and strength, an ever-present help
> in trouble.

We are part of the problem and it will take all of our efforts to help solve it. We are fortunate that God is merciful and will forgive us if we will only repent of our sins and faithfully follow His commandments. I pray that our Lord will give each one of us the strength to carry on and His love will guide us on the narrow road ahead. May His grace and wisdom be a light to keep us looking towards Heaven where tears of sorrow will be replaced with joy and perfect happiness forever and ever! (2 Chronicles 7:13-14)

When I shut up the heavens so that there is no rain, or command locusts to devour the land, or send a plague among my people, if my people, who are called by my name, will humble themselves and pray and seek my face and turn from their wicked ways, then will I hear from heaven and will forgive their sin and will heal their land.

Update – (2010 – 2018) and Beyond

2010 – unemployment has hovered near 10% leaving many people out of work but at least the market has stabilized somewhat. A miracle election held in Massachusetts to replace the late Senator Edward Kennedy, placed the health care bill on hold after the people there elected a Republican which hasn't occurred for several decades. Unfortunately, the Democrats found a controversial way around the close Senate vote to pass the heath care bill in opposition to the will of the people. The people will have the last word at the midterm elections.

2012 – Obama was reelected but election results overall proved to be a disaster for the Democrats who lost the House majority to Republicans and nearly lost their majority in the Senate. In the 2014-midterm elections, Republicans took control of the House and Senate. This I believe was largely due to the unpopularity of Obamacare that turned out to be very expensive leaving many unable to afford health insurance.

2016 – Donald Trump was elected in a major upset over rival Hillary Clinton. It was the Christian vote that made the difference, defying all the polls and experts who claimed it would be nearly impossible for Trump to win. Not only did Trump win, but the House and Senate remained under Republican control. Christians have something to be proud of by electing pro-life leaders to Congress and the White House. Our vote does make a difference and in this case, it actually saves lives! Hopefully, this was a lesson learned for all bureaucrats – if you mess with the people by not upholding Godly principles, you will be replaced!

I never thought in a million years that Donald Trump would be our president and believe me, it has caused myself and others concern at times but so far he has stayed true to his pro-life campaign promise. He has also appointed two conservatives to the Supreme Court, Justice Neil Gorsuch, replacing the late Justice Antonin Scalia along with the hard fought battle to confirm Justice Brett Kavanaugh replacing the retiring Justice Anthony Kennedy. There have also been dozens of conservative federal judges appointed. If the election had gone to Hillary Clinton, this would have never occurred which would have left the Supreme Court with a liberal majority that would have negatively impacted conservative values for generations to come.

The economy seems to be thriving under Trump but I still can't see it continuing long-term unless the government and citizens get debt under control. The Federal Reserve is still subsidizing the economy with super low interest rates which has benefited investors in the stock market and has made obtaining loans easier for consumers and businesses but this has come at a price. It has also forced consumers to invest in riskier investments such as stocks because the returns are too low for more conservative investments such a CD's and savings accounts. This has left many more people vulnerable to a sudden downturn in the economy. Most troubling for future generations, the US national debt is now over $20 trillion.

This was one of the most important elections in our century and it literally took a miracle with the most unlikely person to lead the conservative movement to victory. Two years passed quickly with the 2018 midterm elections ending with the Democrats regaining the House and the Republicans holding onto the Senate which is important for future judicial appointees and even the possibility of another Supreme Court nominee. Time will tell if this answer to our prayers will continue. In the meantime, we must continue to pray for the spiritual health of our nation and the world.

Chapter 10

Conclusion

How Do We Know We're Living a Steadfast Christian Life?

We know we are following the right path when the thought of prayer is no longer a burden but is something that we look forward to. Even when our lives become difficult, we will persevere by refusing to fall into the deception of unbelief, not by our own strength, but through Jesus Christ's.

The Sin of Coveting

Coveting our neighbors is a sin that separates us from the people we are coveting and ultimately from God. If we are struggling financially and a friend calls up to tell us that they just received a promotion at work, we have to be careful not to covet them. Instead, we need to congratulate them on their blessing from God. By becoming envious, we are taking away from our friend's blessing and because of this selfish behavior God may temporarily withhold some of our own blessings. He will also sometimes deliberately bless others around us first as a test. God is more concerned with our soul than material things, and if we fail to have true joy for others, He may withhold our blessing for our own good. I know first hand that it can be extremely hard not to covet others.

We can help others reduce the temptation to covet by being more sensitive to their needs, especially when we know they are struggling with a particular problem. In this situation, it might be better if we hold back revealing our blessing to them to avoid hurting their feelings. God in His perfect wisdom took the sin of coveting serious enough to include it in His commandments. (Exodus 20:17)

> *You shall not covet your neighbor's house. You shall not covet your neighbor's wife, or his manservant or maidservant, his ox or donkey, or anything that belongs to your neighbor.*

Being content with what we have and putting the needs and concerns of others before ourselves is a good way to achieve true happiness, not just for our own satisfaction but rather as an expression of our love for God.

Loving God With All Our Heart
Matthew 22:36-40

> *"Teacher, which is the greatest commandment in the Law?" Jesus replied: " 'Love the Lord your God with all your heart and with all your soul and with all your mind.' This is the first and greatest commandment. And the second is like it: 'Love your neighbor as yourself.' All the Law and the Prophets hang on these two commandments."*

We do this not because we have to but because we want to. As Christians, there should be a noticeable difference in the way we live compared to the secular world. Though we will still face difficulties and great trials along the way, our faith in God will help us overcome these problems.

The term "Christian" is not just a word; rather, it is a way of life that carries with it many responsibilities that should not be taken lightly. Jesus warns us to be vigilant and remain watchful. (Matthew 24:36-39,42-44)

> *No one knows about that day or hour, not even the angels in heaven, nor the Son but only the Father. As it was in the days of Noah, so it will be at the coming of the Son of Man. For in the days before the flood, people were eating and drinking, marrying and giving in marriage, up to the day Noah entered the ark; and they knew nothing about what would happen until the flood came and took them all away. That is how it will be at the coming of the Son of Man.*
>
> *Therefore keep watch, because you do not know on what day your Lord will come. But understand this: If the owner of the house had known at what time of night the thief was coming, he would have kept watch and would not have let his house be broken into. So you also must be ready, because the Son of Man will come at an hour when you do not expect him.*

At a moment's notice we must be willing to give up everything and follow Him. If this is a hard thought to consider, we may not be prepared to meet our Lord. We cannot be like Lot's wife who even after being warned by an angel, looked back at what she had left behind. (Genesis 19:15-17, 24-26)

> *With the coming of dawn, the angels urged Lot, saying, "Hurry! Take your wife and your two daughters who are here, or you will be swept away when the city is punished."*
>
> *When he hesitated, the men grasped his hand and the hands of his wife and of his two daughters and led them safely out of the city, for the LORD was*

merciful to them. As soon as they had brought them out, one of them said, "Flee for your lives! Don't look back, and don't stop anywhere in the plain! Flee to the mountains or you will be swept away!" Then the LORD rained down burning sulfur on Sodom and Gomorrah—from the LORD out of the heavens. Thus he overthrew those cities and the entire plain, including all those living in the cities— and also the vegetation in the land. But Lot's wife looked back, and she became a pillar of salt.

Like many of us, she had become too attached to the sinful place left behind and Scripture tells us that her disobedience resulted in her body turning into a pillar of salt. Once we become committed to God, we cannot look back and must go forward no matter how hard the road ahead may become. This is an excellent reminder that Jesus is responsible for our well being, and if we focus more on eternal things, He will take care of the rest.

Lasting Joy Only Comes From God

True joy can only come from God and we make a big mistake when we only rely on others such as our spouse or friends to make us happy. Placing this burden on loved ones can cause undo stress on the relationship. I've heard it said that a person is not ready for a serious relationship until they really don't need one.

I know in my own life, I made some poor decisions as a teenager that resulted in failed relationships. I disobeyed God and found myself deeply entrenched in the worldly desires of my heart. By doing so, I paid a price that compromised part of my high school years. Through the grace of our Lord, a year into college, and a period of time after graduation, I decided to take a break from dating and instead refocused my attention on God. That decision resulted in some of the best years of my life. It was in those years that I reached a deeper level in my faith which enabled me to develop a strong relationship with Christ. He became my first priority and I found more time to pray, travel, and help others in need.

Big Brother

During that time, I had the opportunity to take youth out on camping trips and share the Lord with them. I also considered myself fortunate when I became a mentor and friend to a young teenage boy whose family had gone through a divorce.

I remember taking him out on random acts of charity. We would go unannounced to several older widows' homes we didn't even know and offer to rake their lawn or repair a damaged item. On one occasion after we had picked some apples for an elderly woman, she came out with some homemade apple pie fresh out of the oven and treated us with her kind words and generous hospitality. I can still remember my young teenage friend's comment, "Helping her out really makes me feel good, I hope we can do this kind of thing more often." On the next stop, we raked the yard of another elderly woman who followed my young friend all around the yard constantly giving him compliments on what a good worker he was and how it was rare to see a boy his age helping others. His smile was so big that he could hardly contain it and I could see some of the pain caused by his parents' divorce slowly lifting off this young man's inner being. He was quickly learning that helping others was very gratifying and it gave me great pleasure to watch both the woman and my friend experience such joy. (Psalm 68:5)

> *A father to the fatherless, a defender of widows, is*
> *God in his holy dwelling.*

I had a lot of good talks with him especially about his father who lived thousands of miles away. I could tell that he really missed him and on one occasion, I took him into an empty church and told him that praying for his dad would make him feel better. It was so quiet in there that it almost hurt and the presence of the Holy Spirit was so powerful that it overwhelmed both of us. Looking over at him while praying, I noticed tears were streaming down his face as he opened up his soul to God. I just quietly waited there praying to our Heavenly Father that He would heal my friend.

When we left, he told me that he really felt good while in the church and could feel God's presence. It was a special moment for him that marked the beginning of his healing process with his dad as well as with his eternal Father. It was also a turning point in my life which brought me closer to Christ by teaching me the power of prayer in all things.

Youth Camping Trip

On one particular camping trip, I had the opportunity to take four teenagers up to Grandpa's goldmine mentioned earlier. Two of them had been getting into trouble so I thought taking them out of the city and into the mountains would help. They all accepted my invitation so I planned the backpacking trip for the upcoming weekend. We left early in the morning and arrived at the camp before noon. It was the first time the boys had been there and they couldn't wait to start hiking to our destination. We used the mining site for a base camp and planned to hike up to a high alpine lake that was full of brook trout. We would set up another camp at that location.

There were two alternate routes that led to our destination. One was shorter but more difficult because of the steepness involved and the other was more level but took an extra hour to get there. We had a vote and it was unanimous to take the shorter route. We loaded up our backpacks with all our provisions and gear and started up the steep rugged trail that went pretty much straight up the mountain peak. We had to rest often because the nearly 13,000- foot altitude was starting to take its toll. About a half hour later we had reached the summit and the views were spectacular. We had a 360-degree vantage point that revealed hundreds of miles of wilderness in all directions. To our north, we caught the first glimpse of the lake where we would be camping out. It was still several miles off in the distance off the other side of the mountain we had just conquered. Fortunately for us the hike down was less steep. We were all so anxious to get there that we went against our better judgment and started to jog down the mountain. Before long, we started to fall and nearly injured ourselves before I conjured up enough sense to slow everyone down.

About halfway there a flock of white-tailed ptarmigans blew up in our faces, giving us a brief scare before we realized what they were. The flock landed a short distance away and we sat down for a moment and watched them strut around foraging for food. Their brownish-white feathers blended in perfectly with the surroundings. It is amazing that these tough alpine birds can survive up there, especially in the wintertime. We then continued on with our journey to the lake that was now only a few minutes away. The boys were already talking about who would catch the first fish, and when we were close enough, they took off running to the water's edge. Off in the distance, I could see that one of them had clearly beaten the others there and already had his fishing pole out of his pack with his first cast well on its way. Then I saw him jumping for joy after he quickly caught his first fish. Instead of setting up camp, we all started fishing and caught our limit soon afterward. Having fresh fish for dinner was a real treat especially after a hard hike.

During the night while everyone was lying in their sleeping bags, I couldn't resist telling them the story of the bear attack that happened long ago at that old bus. I knew it wasn't a nice thing to do but I was pretty ornery back then. They just laughed it off but I could tell it terrified a few of them, especially when I asked one of them if they would go outside to check on our gear. He told one of the other guys to do it and they kept going around in a circle trying to avoid it. I went outside the tent and then quickly came back in screaming in fear which sent them deep inside their sleeping bags. When they finally realized I was only joking, we all had a good laugh.

The next morning came quickly and I was surprised to find that it was lightly raining outside which was not in the forecast. All the boys were still asleep so I decided to wake them up by banging metal pots together. All I got out of them were a few moans and groans but after being persistent they at least became conscious. It was Sunday morning and I thought it would be a good opportunity to have a small church service. When I told them my idea they responded with the usual, "Do we have to?" I told them how ungrateful they were for not giving God a few minutes of their time especially since there wasn't anything else they could be doing in a rain storm. My psychology didn't work and I started to get a little frustrated. I then told them that God would get angry with them if they continued to ignore Him. Immediately afterwards, a huge explosion rocked our tent which sent them deep into their bags in sheer terror. There hadn't been any lightning during the night or in the morning, but at the perfect moment there was a sudden blast that struck directly over our tent. I took full advantage of the opportunity and once again asked if anyone wanted to participate. They all quickly volunteered.

Was it just an accident or was God trying to make a lasting impression on those boys that they wouldn't soon forget? I felt fortunate to have had the time to expose them to God's awesome power. This experience would not have occurred if I was only thinking about my own life. I thank Him for opening up my eyes so I could share time with others, even if I was pretty ornery back then.

Canadian Angel

During that time, my life felt complete with no need to start a relationship with a woman. However, little did I know that God was busy making plans for me. While volunteering at a soup kitchen run by the Missionaries of Charity (late Mother Theresa's order), I met a young Canadian woman who had come down from British Columbia, Canada, to volunteer her time. It had almost been five years since really even noticing a woman but when I first saw her, it was as if my spirit leapt for joy.

Later that evening while lying in an unfamiliar bed, I prayed extremely hard that God would allow me to become better acquainted with her. The next day, the sisters had planned a birthday party for my uncle who has dedicated his life helping out the Missionaries of Charity in their work with the poorest of the poor. His birthday was to take place at a small lake surrounded by tall Ponderosa Pine trees located a few miles out of town. This was also my last chance to get to know the Canadian girl because it was her last day before returning home.

† † †

I had recently been to this lake while taking a group of Navajo Indians up into the hills to track wild turkeys and deer. It was an opportunity for all of us to get out of the city and back into the wilderness where we could experience their native hunting grounds. As soon as we arrived, they jumped out of the truck and were on game trails within minutes. It was refreshing to see how excited they were while out in nature away from all the problems that tear them down. Even more amazing was their ability to take a raw piece of wood and shape it into the form of an animal using only a pocket knife. Their skilled hands and their ability to perceive every detail in their surrounding environment was unmatched. To keep it authentic, I brought some hard-earned elk steaks that I had taken earlier that fall. After the afternoon hike, we fried up some elk steak over a natural fire that turned out to be delicious cooked that way. We first gave thanks to Diyin (God in Navajo) and then we all ripped into the wild meat. For a moment it felt like we were living back several hundred years ago in a time when that type of life was the norm. On that day, I formed a bond with my new friends that would not be broken.

† † †

Because of my positive experience at the lake, I felt optimistic that good things would also happen at my uncle's party. I prayed to have a chance to talk with the Canadian girl and my prayer was answered. Though my conversation with her was brief, I thoroughly enjoyed being in her presence. To my disappointment, the party quickly came to an end and I couldn't get up enough courage to ask for her phone number.

Little did I know that my grandpa, who had come with me to attend his son's birthday party, was watching my every move. He came up and quietly asked me if I had gotten her phone number. When I told him no, he couldn't believe it! In a loud voice he said, "Are you going to just sit there and let her get away? If I were your age, I would've already had her number and gone on our first date!" Grandpa couldn't take it anymore and decided to take matters into his own hands. I remember feeling mortified when he waved her over to where we were standing and abruptly asked for her father's number in case he needed information about British Columbia's real estate prices. Like me, Grandpa was a real estate broker so this old business line worked liked a charm and he felt proud to have helped me out. I had never seen him do anything like that before and wondered why he felt so compelled?

Several weeks later, I gathered enough courage to call which completely caught her by surprise. During our conversation, I found out that she never gave me a second thought after meeting me. Embarrassed, I explained to her how my grandpa had used the real estate thing as an excuse to get her number. To my relief, she thought the whole thing was funny and told me how blessed I was to have such a great grandpa. To make a long story short, after many hours of phone calls, long letters, and eventually meeting in person again on several occasions, we developed a serious relationship and eventually got married. I often referred to her as my Canadian Angel. I thank God daily for bringing us together which has resulted in many years of happiness. However, we have not been immune to the daily struggles of marriage and have had to draw on Christ's strength to make it work out for the best. Despite these trials, I wouldn't trade our marriage for anything.

Looking back over the years, I can clearly see how God has directed my path. When God is in control, things work out for the best. I also thank God for Grandpa who took time out of his life to look after my better interest – if it were not for his persistence, I would have missed out on this wonderful blessing. Though Grandpa has passed away, his memory remains strong in my heart.

Demolition Derby

I didn't always remember Grandpa as being so kind. Back when my brother and I were only four and five years old, we overheard him telling Grandma that he hated his old green car and wanted to get rid of it. We took what he said to heart and when Grandpa left for work, we decided to help out by taking care of it. With hammer in hand, I got inside the driver's seat and started pounding the dash in and everything else that would break. Meanwhile, my brother was more cautious and hid up on the hillside behind some oak brush and started hurling grapefruit-sized rocks at the windshield and body of the car. After a few hours of this, the car was completely destroyed. All along, we felt we were doing Grandpa a favor. He didn't see it that way and when Grandpa came home and saw what had happened, his face turned to a dangerous red and he started screaming. Unfortunately, I was still inside the car working on some finishing touches when he arrived.

Before I could escape from the scene, he spotted me running up the hillside where my brother was already hiding. I had never seen him so angry and he threatened to call the police on me. This scared me half to death. I ended up getting most of the blame because my brother was so sneaky about it that no one saw him. I tried my hardest to include him, but to no avail. Even after years had passed, Grandpa still got mad if anyone mentioned it. I guess a person should be careful what they say – you never know who might be listening.

This wasn't the first time that Grandpa had one of his cars destroyed by family members. When my mom was a young girl, she decided to play in his unattended car parked in their driveway which was located on the edge of a steep drop-off. She managed to disengage the parking brake and shift the car out of gear into neutral, causing the car to start slowly rolling backwards towards the edge of the drop-off. When she realized what was happening, Mom was fortunate enough to safely jump out just before it went over the edge and violently rolled down the steep slope, finally crashing below into a commercial building that Grandpa owned. At first, he was furious when he found out what had happened, but when he found Mom hiding in her closet several hours later with tear-filled eyes, he knew that she had already learned her lesson.

† † †

Trying to surrender my life to God hasn't always been easy. There have been times where my unbelief, fear, and sinful nature have interfered with His will, but I can honestly say that Our Lord Jesus has never let me down and has always picked me up, even if I didn't deserve it. He does this for everyone who follows Him.

God Loves Everyone

Some have commented, "If God knows the future and already knew from the beginning of time that certain people would go to hell then why did He allow them to be born?" While reading excerpts from St. Thomas Aquinas from his Summa Theologica, I found the following response to the comment above:

> *Why, since He knows from eternity which of us will lose our souls, did He make us at all? This question*

is a coward's complaint against his humanity and the share of divinity given to men. If we are to have a chance at Heaven, we must run the risk of hell; no man is in hell who did not have, time after time, the chance of taking Heaven in his grasp. Heaven is worth the risk of hell; God is worth the risk of the Devil.[29]

In other words, God is extremely gracious to give each one of us the opportunity to obtain Heaven. Without being born, the opportunity never existed and as Christians, this is a horrible thought to bear and it sheds light to the complete ignorance of the question.

It is an amazing thought to think that God, with all his mighty power, does not force us to follow Him; instead, He graciously showers us with all the opportunities we need, and in the end, there will be no excuses.

God loves everyone equally from all nations, no matter their religious background or lack thereof. God is far above the walls of religion that separate us on earth and is more interested in the heart, not necessarily the religion one belongs to. I am not saying we should discard our particular denomination or faith or that all faiths are equal; rather, we all need to live out our lives peacefully, lovingly, and with mutual respect for one another (golden rule).

As Christians, we believe in the truth of Jesus Christ, Son of the living God; therefore, if we have been given the opportunity to believe this truth, we have no excuse not to be steadfast in our conviction to uphold the responsibilities of our faith. Those who have not yet learned about the good news of our Lord and people of different faiths, will be judged according to their own merits. (Luke 12:48)

---

29 Farrel, O.P., S.T.M, Walter, and Martin J. Healy, S.T.D. *My Way of Life, Pocket Edition of St. Thomas, The Summa Simplified for Everyone.* NA ed. Brooklyn: Confraternity of the Precious Blood, 1952. 46. Print.

*From everyone who has been given much, much
will be demanded; and from the one who has been
entrusted with much, much more will be asked.*

If we're Christian, we need to live according to Christ's teachings,
not our own modified version. I know this type of philosophy
may be controversial amongst some Christians, especially when
Scripture clearly states that we can only be saved through Jesus
Christ. This is true but it cannot be emphasized enough that it
is Jesus who saves us through His infinite grace and mercy, not
because of who or what we are. (John 14:6)

*Jesus answered, "I am the way and the truth and the
life. No one comes to the Father except through me."*

He knows the heart and will exercise perfect justice and mercy
for everyone. I think there will be a lot of surprises in Heaven.
(Matthew 21:31)

*. . . Jesus said to them, "I tell you the truth, the
tax collectors and the prostitutes are entering the
kingdom of God ahead of you . . . ."*

Accepting God is more involved than just a conscious decision, it
is a way of life. When we take our faith seriously, our lives become
more focused and simple because we remove the obstacles that
can oppose our relationship with God. Our body, soul, and spirit
cannot function properly without a solid relationship with Christ
because this is how we were created. Without this void being filled,
we will be hopelessly lost – dead bones blindly stumbling along,
never finding true happiness; a lonely desperate search that will
never be fulfilled.

Only by choosing God, and only by accepting what we have instead
of what we do not, will we find happiness. If our joy hinges only on
our circumstances, we will be on a constant rollercoaster ride. It
can get to the point where no matter how much we accumulate, we
still want more. That is why it is so important for us as Christians

to be content no matter where we are in life. This can be difficult to put into practice especially if we are not doing very well financially. I'm not saying we shouldn't have dreams to make life better for us and our families; instead, we should be careful not to get lost in the material and lose focus on what really matters.

Learning To Be Content With What We Have

As Christians, we need to be content with what we have and shouldn't try to find false happiness through the excessive accumulation of material things. In our country, Christians are sinking deeper into secularism. What we watch, wear, eat, and participate in partly defines who we are and what we stand for. As Scripture clearly states, we cannot serve two masters – we have to make a choice in whom or what we are going to serve. God has given us a free will, and if we choose Him, we must be willing to commit to his ways, not our own modified version.

If we can just learn to be thankful, no matter what our situation, we won't always be looking to the past or the future for our happiness – we can have it right now. If our situation isn't going very well, we can rejoice in the fact that Christ will soon deliver us from our problem. If everything is good, we can praise Him for what he has given us. We need to accept our present situation and find happiness in the now, instead of longing for better things in the future.

When we are younger, we cannot wait to be older, and when in high school, we cannot wait to be in college or begin our careers, and when we start our careers, we dream of making more money, and when we make more money, our expectations increase so we need more money to satisfy our desires, and then the thought of retiring keeps us going, and when we retire, we dream about our youth, and so on. This is completely contrary to God's intentions for us – He wants us to rejoice in everything, big and small, good or bad. If we only live for another time other than the present, we will never catch up to the joy we are pursuing. (Philippians 4:11-13)

> *I am not saying this because I am in need, for I have learned to be content whatever the circumstances. I know what it is to be in need, and I know what it is to have plenty. I have learned the secret of being content in any and every situation, whether well fed or hungry, whether living in plenty or in want. I can do everything through him who gives me strength.*

What is Really Important in Life?

We need to pray and ask God for the wisdom to recognize what is truly important; family, health, friendships, and most importantly, our relationship with Jesus Christ. Sometimes it is obvious when we neglect these responsibilities, like when a father rarely attends his son's basketball games because his own personal goals overshadow his responsibilities as a father, or when a member of the family refuses to go to church with the excuse that everyone who goes is a hypocrite. But isn't the main purpose for going to church to have communion with God? Therefore, we shouldn't let the actions of other people be the deciding factor on whether or not we attend.

Other situations can be more difficult to discern and require wisdom from God. For example, should a family do whatever it takes to allow a mom to stay home and raise their children, even if it could mean selling their larger home for a smaller, less expensive one? How much should we be willing to sacrifice for the well being of our children?

Choosing to be a stay-at-home mom can be very challenging in our present times and may never become a reality for some. In our society, most families have become dependant on two incomes which requires a significant change in lifestyle to enable a mom to stay at home. Working at home may be the best way to achieve this goal but these types of jobs are hard to come by. After we were married and had our first son, my wife while attending nursing school, changed her career in mid stream to become a medical transcriptionist. She did this to be able to work at home. Early in our marriage, we were also fortunate to be able to live in a home for several years that I managed for a generous couple. This enabled us to cut our costs which helped allow my wife to stay at home with our son when we were first starting out.

Even though we may not be able to find a way to be there for our children, there is no situation that God cannot figure out, and if we trust in Him, He will lead us in the right direction. Parents are the first line of defense in protecting their children and every option available must be considered.

Update, July 2009 – Hike to Grandpa's Goldmine and Beyond

This book wouldn't be complete without first making a long-awaited visit to Grandpa's goldmine located high in the rugged Rocky Mountains. It has been over 17 years since I've made the trip up there – man does time fly by!

I finished up a much needed job and decided to celebrate by taking my family on a day hike that didn't appear too hard when looking at the map. The journey would begin by driving up a steep four-wheel drive road to Grandpa's mine. From there we would embark on a ten-mile, round trip adventure to a high alpine lake I had never been to but had always wanted to see. I invited one of my teenage cousins to come along and he eagerly accepted. Like myself, he is really into nature photography and this would provide him with an opportunity for some spectacular pictures. The last time I had been on this trail was when I took some of my cousins and other youth camping as described earlier in this chapter. That was a long time ago when I was much younger. I wondered how I would hold up nearly 20 years later.

We left at 7:00 a.m. and arrived at the mine two hours later. I had forgotten just how beautiful this high mountain valley was. There were still patches of snow melting from the warm summer sun which caused icy cold water to quickly race down the steep mountain side. Moments after loading up our day packs and starting on our hike, I noticed a large herd of elk crossing a patch of snow about a quarter of a mile above our trail. There stood over fifty elk consisting mostly of cows and their calves and a few bulls lingering behind. The elk were directly above Grandpa's goldmine. To me, this was the real treasure.

Within minutes we reached the mine and boy what a difference a few decades had made. The old bus we once used as a camp had become an aluminum shell with only small rodents and ground squirrels now using it for their home. I told everyone the story of when the bear tried to break in but was quickly reminded that they had already heard it many times before. The goldmine had been broken into and a large metal door that Grandpa had built to keep people out was lying on the ground. Someone obviously hooked a metal chain to it and yanked it out with their truck. They must have been disappointed when they didn't find any gold bars, but instead some old timbers and a vertical shaft full of water. After taking some pictures and reminiscing a bit, we continued up the trail on our journey to the lake.

Full of anticipation, we hardly noticed the moderately steep uphill climb that led to the upper trail located on the top edge of a deep narrow canyon with a vertical drop of nearly a thousand feet. The scenery was spectacular in all directions. It was truly inspiring to be up there above timberline in God's country. Across the other side of the canyon, we spotted another herd of elk feeding on a lush steep slope. After taking some pictures of the beautiful scenery, we continued up the now gently sloping trail that led to our destination. Even though it was gentle, we could feel the effects of high altitude as we approached the 13,000-foot level. It was a crystal clear day with a strong breeze from the north that helped cool us off in the near 80-degree temperature.

The trail led to the head of the canyon which was rimmed by

13,000-foot peaks in which we would have to walk around to get to the lake. It was intimidating to say the least but little by little we kept making progress.

We kept walking and walking and the views kept getting better and better. The gorgeous mountain flowers were in full bloom and were all around us. They were arranged perfectly as if someone had landscaped this beautiful scene. After hiking for a few hours, about three-quarters of the way to our destination, we finally made it around to the south edge of a basin where we were pleasantly surprised to find another wider canyon that showcased two magnificent jagged peaks. They jutted from the canyon floor and towered over the surrounding mountains. At first we could only see their tops, but as we made it to the crest of the high alpine ridge they came into full view and took our breath away. This was truly an incredible sight. I had been to this overlook once before while hiking with my uncle and his wife but had forgotten how beautiful it was.

On my previous trip the sky was completely overcast and the towering peaks were partially obscured by thick cloud cover. We were caught in a fierce lightning-rain-hail-snow-windstorm. This location is high atop the alpine tundra with nowhere to take cover. The storm came on quickly and all we could do was squat down and place our heads between our knees and pray that the violent lightning striking all around wouldn't hit us. I could see chunks of debris flying through the air as the lightning struck the ground only a hundred feet away. My hair was full of static electricity and I thought for sure I was going to die. The rain and snow mixture wasn't so bad but when it turned into hail, the piercing sting on the top of my head, neck, and back was very painful. It was an experience that will not be forgotten.

Just as quickly as it started the storm ended and the sun came out which helped to warm my cold drenched body. I found my uncle's wife nearby but my uncle ran down into the steep canyon and had become disoriented during the storm. We started yelling for him and after a short while, he answered back and I thanked God we were all safe. We hurried back down the trail to avoid getting caught in another storm. I learned the hard way that you don't go up into the high country without being well prepared.

† † †

From that point forward I was in unfamiliar territory on our journey to the lake. I had to rely on my map to continue on towards our destination. We had to leave the comfort of the trail and things started to get a little out of control. We had already been hiking for several hours and were getting tired. We came to a small overlook and without knowing it, my cousin decided to slide down a long steep patch of snow to get to the bottom more quickly. According to my son who was watching him, he did fine until reaching the bottom but couldn't stop his momentum, causing him to tumble into an uncontrolled summersault onto the dry rocky ground before finally coming to a hard stop. When he signaled that he was ok, my son started laughing hysterically as he said it was one of the funniest things he had ever seen. I went over to make sure he was ok and lucky for him, my cousin came out of it with only a small scratch. If he had broken a bone, it would have been nearly impossible to get him out of there without a search and rescue team.

About half an hour later, we came around a corner and there it was; a beautiful emerald blue lake tucked into a small basin with slide rock on its western bank with brush and wild grasses around the rest. I couldn't wait to get down there and catch one of the native cutthroat trout the lake was famous for. We found a nice grassy area along the edge of the lake to have a well-earned lunch. After sitting down, we all realized how tired we were from the nearly four-hour hike. Fishing would have to wait for a few more minutes as I lay on my back staring at the nearly cloudless blue sky thanking our Lord for allowing us to witness such a beautiful place. After a short while, I couldn't wait any longer and invited everyone to go fishing with me. At first we were a little disappointed as nothing would bite our spinners. My son and cousin, bored from the lack of action, decided to take turns sliding down a nearby patch of snow. My wife just lay there and read a book.

After experimenting for a while with little luck, I finally figured out what they were interested in. It took a small spinner with a slow steady retrieve to catch some of the most beautiful fish I'd ever seen. They had bright red bellies and of course the classic reddish-orange slit under their gills, hence their name, cutthroat trout. After catching and releasing a dozen fish, my legs were fatigued so I joined my wife who was still reading her book. I just lay there for the next hour relaxing, trying to regain the necessary strength needed for the return trip. At one point, I briefly entertained the thought of setting up a makeshift camp to spend the night there. We didn't have enough food or gear but the thought of not having to go back so soon was tempting. I halfheartedly mentioned it to everyone but the idea was quickly rejected. No one wanted to go through a below freezing night without a sleeping bag and I didn't blame them. After having a good rest, we loaded up our gear and headed back.

About halfway to our car, my legs started cramping and even the pads on our dog's paws formed blisters and started tearing open. The round trip was just too long for one day and I knew the balance of the hike would be a rough one. With about a mile to go, our dog just sat on the trail and wouldn't move anymore even after we called her. My wife inspected her paws and noticed that her blisters were getting worse. She had been running all over the place the entire trip and probably traveled five times the distance we had. I decided to pick her up and carry her the rest of the way;

she didn't mind being slung around on the top of my shoulders one bit. Unfortunately for me, fatigue started setting in and I didn't know if I could make it with the extra weight. My son and cousin with all their youthful energy had walked well ahead of us and were already at the car. I told them earlier to not get too far ahead in case something happened to either of us, but you know how teenagers are.

Despite being completely exhausted from the long hike back, we made it safely to the car. However, my wife and I had pushed ourselves to the limit and for the next several days, we could barely walk. It was well worth it to be able to witness, up close and personal, our Lord's creation which refreshed our minds and renewed our souls. I hope to return again soon to the mine – this beautiful place that Grandpa left for us to enjoy. This experience was a wonderful break from our stressful world.

The purity of the wilderness helps to give a fresh perspective on life because all the distractions of daily living are removed long enough for us to see things more clearly – in a more positive light. Pictures from this hike can be found at my website at www. steadfastchristian.com.

God is The Only Way

As Christians, if we do not seek our Lord we will not have lasting joy. And no matter how much we accumulate in this life, we will never be satisfied because the desires of our hearts can only be filled by Christ. Nothing in this world, no matter its importance, can compare to our relationship with God. He doesn't want us to love Him for what He gives us but rather, for who He is. Our blessings should not be the primary reason for our love; therefore, only one thing should be important – eternal life in God's holy presence which begins here on Earth. The only thing that should be feared is sin because sin separates us from God.

In the turbulent times in which we live, we cannot be overcome with fear and anxiety. When we listen to the news and hear about failing economies, pestilences, and wars taking place throughout the world, we must realize that God is in complete control with nothing that goes unnoticed by Him. However, this does not relieve us from our obligation to pray for our leaders who are in need of divine wisdom to lead us through these dangerous times. Through prayer, God has allowed us to become integral participants in the future direction of our world but we can never forget that God is the one in charge. The power of prayer should not be underestimated and its use should not be limited.

When faced with a trial, we need to look back on our lives and remember all the times that God has been faithful to us. Let's face it – Jesus has never let us down and isn't about to stop now. We often think our present trials are more difficult than the ones from our past and therefore, think God will not be able to help us in our present dilemma. We have to quit limiting God's power. There is nothing too big or small for Him to handle and there is nothing He won't do to lift us up and save us in our time of need.

God had to constantly remind ancient Israel what He had done for them because they had little faith, just as we have little faith today. (Micah 6:4,5)

> "My people, what have I done to you? How have I burdened you? Answer me.
>
> I brought you up out of Egypt
>
> and redeemed you from the land of slavery. I sent
>
> Moses to lead you,
>
> also Aaron and Miriam. My people, remember
>
> what Balak king of Moab counseled

and what Balaam son of Beor answered. Remember
your journey from Shittim to Gilgal,

that you may know the righteous acts of the

LORD."

Keeping a prayer journal is a good way to remember what our Lord has done for us. The knowledge acquired from our past will help build up our confidence in the present and future. This in turn will help to lessen our fear and anxiety when trouble comes our way. Only God can give us the strength to overcome our fears. It requires that we first believe in Him and then we can learn to trust.

As Christians, we have to quit playing games with our faith and make a real stand for Christ. Jesus needs workers now more than ever – souls are at stake and the battle for them has intensified. As they say in baseball, it's time to step up to the plate. If you miss the first pitch, make an adjustment – don't just repeat the same bad swing, choke up a little, step back in the batter's box, move closer to the plate – do whatever it takes to increase your chances for getting a hit. The same is true for Christians – we have to do whatever it takes to stay focused on God.

Jesus warns us to stay awake and be ready for His coming and the only way to do this is to live our lives in prayer. We have to get out of our comfort zones and reach out to those who are less fortunate and who are rejected by society. We need to encourage one another instead of tearing each other down through gossip and unkind words. We do these good things most importantly for our Lord whom we love.

Fear should not be our motivating factor to do good works. It should not be a burden but rather a privilege to serve our Lord. To be lukewarm in our faith is a mistake because it also robs us from the full potential that Christ has intended for each of our lives. Young, old, and everyone in between must become living examples of Christ's love in a world that has gone astray and is in desperate need of God.

The end of this book is really just the beginning of my family's journey with Christ. As Christians, we need to come together and let each other know that we are not alone in our struggles to remain steadfast in our belief. This challenge may seem monumental at times but giving up is not an option. My dad always taught me to never say "can't," but instead "can't hardly" (difficult but possible). Can't hardly provides for a way out and this simple yet powerful expression from my dad has helped me overcome many problems in my life. As a result, I have tried to remove can't from my vocabulary.

Combining this with God's Word, nothing is impossible, no challenge too great, no trial too difficult to overcome. The only thing holding us back is our lack of faith in Christ's ability to solve our problems. The following Scripture is one of my favorites because Jesus tells us how easy it is to approach Him for help and just how ridiculous we are when we don't trust in Him with our petitions. (Luke 11:9-13)

> "So I say to you: Ask and it will be given to you; seek and you will find; knock and the door will be opened to you. For everyone who asks receives; he who seeks finds; and to him who knocks, the door will be opened."

> "Which of you fathers, if your son asks for a fish, will give him a snake instead? Or if he asks for an egg, will give him a scorpion? If you then, though you are evil, know how to give good gifts to your children, how much more will your Father in heaven give the Holy Spirit to those who ask him!"

Our Lord's sense of humor in the second half of this Scripture is refreshing which makes me smile every time I read it. His promise here is life changing if we will only listen to Him and believe by becoming steadfast in our faith and walk with Christ.

Finale

I will close with a finale of important Scriptures.

(Psalm 46:1-3,7), (1 Corinthians 4:20), (2 Timothy 3:1-9,14-17), (John 16:33), (Matthew 28:18-20)

> *God is our refuge and strength, an ever-present help in trouble.*
>
> *Therefore we will not fear, though the earth give way and the mountains fall into the heart of the sea, Though its waters roar and foam and the mountains quake with their surging. Selah*
>
> *The LORD Almighty is with us; the God of Jacob is our fortress. Selah.*
>
> *For the kingdom of God is not a matter of talk but of power.*
>
> *But mark this: There will be terrible times in the last days. People will be lovers of themselves, lovers of money, boastful, proud, abusive, disobedient to their parents, ungrateful, unholy, without love, unforgiving, slanderous, without self-control, brutal, not lovers of the good, treacherous, rash, conceited, lovers of pleasure rather than lovers of God—having a form of godliness but denying its power. Have nothing to do with them.*
>
> *But as for you, continue in what you have learned and have become convinced of, because you know those from whom you learned it, and how from infancy you have known the holy Scriptures, which*

are able to make you wise for salvation through faith in Christ Jesus. All Scripture is God-breathed and is useful for teaching, rebuking, correcting and training in righteousness, so that the man of God may be thoroughly equipped for every good work.

"I have told you these things, so that in me you may have peace. In this world you will have trouble. But take heart! I have overcome the world."

Then Jesus came to them and said, "All authority in heaven and on earth has been given to me. Therefore go and make disciples of all nations, baptizing them in the name of the Father and of the Son and of the Holy Spirit, and teaching them to obey everything I have commanded you. And surely

I am with you always, to the very end of the age."

Ending Prayer

Dear Heavenly Father,

Please send us your Holy Spirit to help us discern what is most pleasing to you. Please awaken your sainthood in each one of us and clothe us in your precious blood, protecting us from all evil. Give us your strength to forgive, to love, to serve, to pray, and to strive to be perfect as You are perfect. Forgive us for all our sins, whether intentional or through our ignorance, and help empower us to live a steadfast Christian life. We ask this in your Son's most precious name, Jesus Christ – Amen

2 Timothy 4:7,8

I have fought the good fight, I have finished the race, I have kept the faith. Now there is in store for

me the crown of righteousness, which the Lord, the righteous Judge, will award to me on that day—and not only to me, but also to all who have longed for his appearing.

About the Author

Patrick Dillon loves the outdoors and spends as much time as possible out enjoying it. His favorite pastime is taking his small fishing boat out on "the lake" with his family, spending a warm summer's day fishing, swimming, and just relaxing. Coaching baseball is a close second. He also enjoys nature photography and time spent exploring the natural world.

He graduated from college with a combined bachelor's degree in environmental science and real estate finance. He followed his dad's and grandpa's footsteps with a career in general contracting combined with real estate, respectively. He continues with his studies in science as a hobby and is passionate about the well being of his faith, family, and country. Patrick and his family currently reside in the beautiful Rocky Mountains of Colorado.

For more information, pictures, requests, suggestions, contact info, and updates, please visit his website @ www.steadfastchristian.com.

www.ingramcontent.com/pod-product-compliance
Lightning Source LLC
Chambersburg PA
CBHW021826090426
42811CB00032B/2047/J